MAN IN HIS THEATRE

MAN IN HIS THEATRE

BY

SAMUEL SELDEN

CHAPEL HILL

The University of North Carolina Press

Manufactured in the United States of America

TO EMILY

I wish to acknowledge my indebtedness to the Alumni Giving Funds made available to and administered by the University Research Council for generous aid in the publication of this book, and to the Ford Foundation for a grant under its program for assisting American university presses in the publication of works in the humanities and the social sciences.

S. S.

Foreword

The present period of the arts in this country belongs very much to the critics. The tables in our homes and the shelves of our libraries are filled not only with books and periodicals by critics but also with works by critics of critics —critics writing on the subject of critics. Commentarial writing has developed so extensively and into such a closed form that many spectators, auditors and readers today are giving more of their time to the perusal of judicial statements on works of art than they are to the original works themselves. I was recently made aware of the layers of criticism that can pile on top of each other when I picked up a volume on my desk—a volume which a reviewer described as "brilliant and important"—and noted in a chapter on *Hamlet* how the author (the principal critic) built his discussion on the back of another man (the second critic) who in turn was probing the mind of still another man (a third critic) under him. The issue which the three stacked critics were arguing was a question as to whether or not Shakespeare's play, granted its long popularity, was not really in part an "artistic failure." This rather intriguing subject would seem to be a large one to treat in the absence of primary material, yet I found that the forty-six pages given to the battle of critical minds included just one and one-half pages from the text of *Hamlet*.

In the past fifty years theatre has had its very full share of intellectual going over. Most of it has been valuable; one will admit this readily and gladly. This body of criticism has greatly helped artists, playgoers, and students to a keener understanding of the lively world of footlights. There has existed another body of criticism, however—one created by unimaginative, "overscholarly" minds—about which one is tempted to wonder if it has not obscured its subject rather than illumined it. George Pierce Baker once observed that in its essence the business of theatre is to find the "shortest path between emotions and emotions." Yet emotions appear to be the last thing to be dealt with in most of our commentaries. We see a score of treatises on "the playwright as thinker" to one on "the playwright as poet."

It has seemed to me that every one of us—craftsman, spectator, general reader, and critic—needs from time to time to re-examine the theatre freshly. We need to rediscover the roots, then the sprouts of drama where they push up, not through the clean pages of books, but through the earthy stuff of life. The primary sciences and history have as much to do with our understanding of theatre as have literary records and literary evaluations. Biology, looking at the living ways of moving, struggling creatures, even the little Protozoa, can tell us much about the reasons for the existence of our playhouses. The records of the ways of human beings can tell us more.

Man in His Theatre is a book of re-exploration. It starts with a brief viewing of animal and human behavior, then it looks at man more closely with respect to his three great fundamental drives: to exercise his human powers, to preserve them, and to extend them. It shows him as a *feeling organism,* yearning to make the best use of his existence. It explains how man's urges long ago created rituals and myths and how the marriage of these two made early drama, and this union continues to influence both the form and the spirit of our present-day theatre.

Man in His Theatre was not written to formulate any special system of thinking. Its whole aim is to help stimulate a new awareness of dramatic forces. My hope is that the book will provoke in those who read it, whatever may be their connection with theatre, a desire to do some further exploring of their own into regions which are filled with exciting challenge but which until now have not, perhaps, had nearly enough attention.

S. S.

Contents

MAN IN HIS THEATRE

We wipe the tears from your eyes that you may see the sun.

From an old Indian ceremonial

I. *Oxytricha*

ON A LITTLE PALLET outside a bark hut lies a Navajo child. His fevered breathing is labored and painful. He is very ill. His mother squats in the shadows watching anxiously while his father moves around him chanting a ritual of healing. Turning his face toward the east, toward the abode of Talking God, the health-giving sun, he prays:

In Kininaékai,
In the house made of dawn,
Oh, Talking God!
His feet, my feet, restore.
His limbs, my limbs, restore.
His body, my body, restore.
His mind, my mind, restore.
His voice, my voice, restore.
His plumes, my plumes, restore.
With beauty before him, with beauty before me.
With beauty behind him, with beauty behind me.
With beauty around him, with beauty around me.
With pollen beautiful in his voice, with pollen
beautiful in my voice.

He bends over the body of the suffering child and intones softly:

It is finished in beauty.
It is finished in beauty.[1]

If the little boy lives he will never become a great warrior. He is not a prince. He will not be a chief of his tribe, and he will probably never own a big house and large flocks. Why then is it important that he should not die? If one would ask the child he would whisper only that he wanted to run again with the other boys, to use his bow and arrows, to play with his dog. If one would ask his mother she would say that he is very dear to her and that if he were not with her there would be an emptiness in her. If one would ask the father he would answer that his son is a part of him, that all he does, all he works for, is for his son. If the little boy were gone there would be nothing to look forward to.

The desire for existence is a strange thing. It is not logic. It is merely a longing. It cannot be explained and it cannot be resisted. It moves as a tremendous power in all creatures, from the largest to the smallest.

Among the Protozoa, the lowliest citizens of the animal world, exists a tiny creature called Oxytricha.[2] It is composed of just one oval-shaped cell with a slit for a mouth and a fringe of little hairs with which it moves. Oxytricha is so small that if its length were multiplied a hundred times it would scarcely reach one inch. Minute as this creature is, though, it has a resolute will to live. Its home is a fresh-water pond. When it senses no harm near, Oxytricha paddles leisurely this way and that, looking for the bacteria on which it feeds or enjoying simply the sensation of swimming. But when there is danger, Oxytricha acts differently. For instance, if it is brought from the pond to a human laboratory and placed in a glass trough under a microscope and one end of this trough is warmed over a burner, the little animal becomes excited. Its hairs begin to lash the water and it darts forward. If it swims into the more heated area, it backs up, takes a quarter turn to the right, and tries again. If it still moves into a danger area, it backs up a second time and makes another attempt to the right. This it continues to do until it can go straight forward into safety.

In a rudimentary way, tiny Oxytricha and the cool and hot water in which it swims represent the first two facts of existence. First, there is an organism which has some powers of action—such as breathing, eating, and paddling in a pond—which it takes pleasure in exercising and which it wishes very much to preserve; and second, there is an environment which offers to the organism's activity both aids and hurts. Oxytricha wants to continue to breathe, eat, and paddle. It finds that there are around it forces that will help its actions, but also some which will hinder them. It must overcome the harmful forces or it will cease to have pleasure in its action at all. It will die.

Oxytricha derives its peculiar desire to preserve its existence, not from anything it learns, but from the nature of that mysterious substance of which it, like all other animal creatures, is made—protoplasm. Just what causes the vitality of this amazing substance no one knows. In its most elementary form, such as the amoeba (one evolutionary half-step below Oxytricha), protoplasm is a microscopic bit of watery translucent stuff quite unimpressive in its appearance. Without the trace of a brain, legs, eyes, or nerves, this speck of jelly nevertheless shows all the principal properties of animal life. It moves: it alters its shape, spreading itself out or tightening itself up into a ball; it shifts itself from place to place. It is responsive to its surroundings: it expands in a friendly environment and contracts in an unfriendly one; it approaches food and withdraws from the point of an electric needle. It turns what it eats into heat, energy, and more protoplasm. It excretes what it cannot use. It breathes. It reproduces itself. It performs with a kind of primitive intelligence every one of the functions necessary to prolong its own existence and assure a future for its kind. Tiny as it is, the speck shows quite clearly a passionate love of life and a purpose to extend it as far as it can.[3]

The most remarkable things about protoplasm are its energy and its capacity for organization. It is a vigorous thing; it fights against extinction. It senses in its elemental way that the universe in which it exists is a place of struggling forces and it tries to do something about its relationship to these. It gathers together its little resources. It orders them for the discharge of functions. It arranges itself for effective living. "The fundamental fact in biology. . . ," says Herbert J. Muller in *Science and Criticism,* "is the organism. The cell is a chemical compound but more significantly a type of biological organization; the whole organism is not a mere aggregate but an architecture."[4] Nowhere is the ordering ability of protoplasm seen more clearly than in the process of growth. The biological scientist, Edmund W. Sinnott, states in *Cell and Psyche* that each living creature is "an *organized* system, each part or quality so related to all the rest that in its growth the individual marches on through a series of specific steps to a specific end or culmination, maintaining throughout its course a delicately balanced state of form and function which tends to restore itself if it is altered."[5]

He illustrates this building genius of cells with a description of the development of an animal embryo. "The fertilized egg of a salamander is cleft into two cells by a vertical wall, then into four as one would quarter an apple, then horizontally into eight, and so on and on. If to our vision these changes are speeded up by time-lapse photography we can witness how the tiny group of cells, through continued cleavage, forms a partly hollow, spherical body; how the upper portion grows down over the yolk mass; how at one point the sphere is pushed in to make the primitive mouth; how above this the puckered neural folds mark out the position of the spinal axis; how they grow over to meet and form the neural tube; how at the sides the primitive gills appear; and how, step after step, the embryo moves swiftly on to form the young larva from which the mature salamander grows. Here is no random process but a steady march, each event in step with the rest as though to a definite and predetermined end. One gets an impression of some unseen craftsman who knows what he is about and who molds the mass of growing cells according to a precise plan. The young salamander seems to go through, before our eyes, an active progress toward a destination in a way which suggests its later movements of behavior, and not a merely passive unfolding. Here seems to be the expression in development of a constantly operating control which from the start and through all its precise steps from egg to adult maintains the embryo as an organized system."[6]

What is more striking than what takes place under favorable conditions is what happens when orderly conditions are disturbed. When, for example, one of the first cells of a salamander embryo is killed, the other develops into a whole animal—not a half, as might be expected. When two fertilized eggs are made to fuse by artificial means, they produce one salamander instead of two. Seemingly, the protoplasm in the cells is guided by some kind of force of direction which induces them to change their regular plan of growth to fit the altered circumstances.

Inherent in protoplasm is a primordial longing to do more than just be; the protoplasm *wants to become.* What it wants to achieve is a state of greater, more effective organization. Stirred by a power of which it cannot be aware, it tries to organize its potentialities. It has an urge to improve itself. The first speck shapes itself into an oval, forms a mouth, and adds a fringe of cilia. It has become Oxytricha (or some similar Protozoan).[7] Now it can swim, seek nourishment, and escape danger more efficiently than it did before. But it is still not satisfied. After some thousands of years of trial and error it finds a way to enlarge its body by multiplying its single cell. Then it develops different kinds of cells: certain ones especially fitted for feeling, others for doing—some for locomotion, some for eating, some for excreting, some for breathing. At later stages of progress it grows fins, gills, special organs of sense, and a central nervous system. Then it gets legs, feet, toes, fingers, and increasingly specialized organs for seeing, hearing, tasting, and smelling. These make it still easier for the protoplasmic organism to survive and to extend its energies.

But meeting the problem of living requires more than the building of the organism itself. It demands also some management of the surroundings. In order to bring the beneficial and the hurtful forces around it under control, each organism must create or modify certain other objects.

What action it takes differs, of course, with different needs. So that it may have shelter for its body, the beetle digs a hole. So that it may catch something to eat, the spider spins a web. So that it may have a place for the rearing of its young, the sparrow builds a nest. So that it may have both protection and comfort for itself and its companions, the beaver constructs a dam. Also it cuts and stores wood for its winter meals. The bee builds a hive. It forms a comb and fills it with honey. The ant makes a hill. The squirrel hoards acorns.

The beetle, the spider, the sparrow, the beaver, the bee, the ant, and the squirrel are masses of protoplasm systematized for survival and growth, and energized by a desire to go on. In this respect they are like Oxytricha. The only difference lies in the fact that the beetle and his companions are larger, many-celled, and far more complex in their structure than the little Protozoan. Vastly different as the bigger animals are from the smaller with respect to form, they share with them the basic elements and feelings of a protoplasmic existence. Both the beetle and Oxytricha are made of a restless substance ever in process of change. No act of will can stop the process. The change must go on. If it stops, the animal dies.

The upward pathway of evolution is a very long one. At the top is man: the Navajo boy and his parents, the school teacher down the road, the President in Washington. Man stands above the beasts, not because the protoplasm of which he is composed is essentially unlike theirs and not because his longing to fulfill its potentialities is different, but only because the substance and the desire in him are better ordered to deal in a *varied* way with the man himself and with the world around him. Like Oxytricha he wants to exist and to exist well. Like Oxytricha he wants to unite himself with beneficial forces and to avoid the harmful. Man achieves these desires much more efficiently because he has better means. He has the service of arms, legs, and organs of many kinds. He can see, hear, touch, taste, and smell. Like Oxytricha he can turn to the right, but unlike Oxytricha he can also turn to the left.

The British biologist E. S. Russell says in *The Directiveness of Organic Activities:* "We have reached the conclusion that directiveness and creativeness are fundamental characteristics of life, shared by no inorganic system; . . . that human directiveness and purposiveness in thought and action are a specialized development of the directiveness and creativeness inherent in life."[8] Protoplasmic life is not aimless; it is motivated, guided by a force of orderliness reaching toward a goal—a higher state of effective organization.

The greatest development in man lies in that part of him called his "brain." Through the millions of years since the time of man's one-cell ancestor the first little threads of more sensitive protoplasm have slowly evolved into nerve fibres, then into small networks of nerves, then into larger networks. These have developed into a whole system of chief and secondary reference points integrated around one principal center. In a marvelously complex way the brain evaluates the impressions of the environment which come to it, checks them against the record of similar impressions in the past, cross-checks these against the results of action taken in response to them, then renders a decision on a new action in accordance with circumstances.

In man this agent has reached such a high state of development that it can now carry on its own activity for long periods almost without consulting the body out of which it grew and to which it is still attached. With all the wonderful power it boasts, however, it has not been able to alter even slightly the basic facts of biological nature. Like the beasts, man remains a vulnerable, essentially physical creature in a world of unstable forces. Like his animal relatives he enjoys the sensation of being alive, and like them he strives constantly and often desperately to adjust himself and his environment in such a way as to keep whole that feeling. Like the little beetle he is driven to keep his body warm and dry. Like the spider he is pushed to satisfy his hunger. Like the sparrow he is impelled to reproduce himself in children and to guard them lovingly during their helpless infancy.

Edmund Sinnott points out that biological organization and psychical activity are fundamentally the same thing. Without the body, without its protoplasmic hungers and impulses, brain would have no reason for being. "Body and mind are simply two aspects of the same biological phenomenon. The first is no more real than the second, for they are one. The pulling together of matter into an organized living system is what we feel as a mental experience."[9] Says E. S. Russell, "We draw no hard and fast line between organic and psychological activity . . . life and mind are at bottom the same."[10]

Since man's physical and mental activities are intimately related, all his aspirations, all his purposes, are bound to both. Even the noblest of his feelings is firmly rooted in the regulatory behavior of the protoplasm of which he is composed. "The whole conscious life of man, rich in ideas, in inspirations, in intellectual subtleties, in imagination and emotion, is simply the manifestation of an organized biological system raised to its loftiest levels."[11]

Throughout his vast activity, man is moved by three great passionate urges:

> To exercise his powers (use his capacities),
> To preserve his powers,
> To enlarge his powers.

Of these three the first is basic. Man shares the urge to exercise his powers with all other living creatures. The existence of that desire is the first fact of living. If Oxytricha were not moved to swim about in the water, or the spider to spin a web, or the beetle to dig in the earth, and if it did not in its elemental way take satisfaction in the action of its little body while doing this, it would not exist long. Each animal has its own peculiar powers and these it *must* use if it is to maintain a feeling of well-being. The powers press to be exercised. The wild bird restrained in a cage yearns to fly. The dog chained to his kennel howls for release—even when he knows he is well-protected and well-fed and has no practical need for running and scenting.

Man has many powers. First are, of course, the ones generally common to animal life, such as breathing, eating, and mating. Then there are the powers of bodily movement and sensation enjoyed in a more complex way, such as those involved in primitive hunting and dancing, or, if a person is more cultivated, in fencing, riding, viewing the beauty of a landscape, and tasting good wine. These powers, all associated somehow with a feeling of effective living, have a special urge if the man has a physical, sensuous temperament and has developed a skill in certain patterns of action which satisfy his hunger. Beyond these are other, even more complicated powers involving psychological factors. A woman takes pride in her cooking; her daughter has pleasure in her piano playing. Her son cherishes his abilities in sonic engineering, and her husband, perhaps, his prowess in breeding hunting dogs. To each person, his powers are precious; they are an integral part of his personality. When, because of illness or of some other block, he cannot use certain of his capacities, he feels, to the extent of that loss, inanimate, "dead."

An old, deaf and widowed schoolteacher now works long hours as a housekeeper in a hotel. She must rise early to count sheets and towels and see that bathrooms are clean and shades are drawn. She has no children, no friends, no hopes for the future. Why does she hold onto her fragment of life? A crippled derelict pokes around the garbage cans of a restaurant for scraps of food and begs drinks from passersby. Why does he, month after month, refrain from taking that one leap off the dock end into the river which would stop his pain? No one can tell, there can only be surmise. Perhaps the deaf woman still takes pleasure in sensing in her fingers the touch of crisp, clean cloths and takes some little pride in her ability to keep humble objects in order. Perhaps the crippled man thinks of the warmth of sunshine and the sound of human voices. He loves them and his capacity for responding to them. He cannot bear to leave them behind.

Those powers which are essential to a man's feeling of well-being he will seek strongly to preserve. The dearer they are to him, the harder he will struggle for them against every force which attacks them. Some of his striving will be involuntary, some of it will be deliberative, but behind all of it will be vigorous compulsion. The man's whole sense of pleasurable existence depends on the feeling that his powers are safe and free. The Indian mother wants to care for her child; the pianist wishes to continue her playing.

But preservation alone is not enough. If the powers are to be used to their uttermost, they must be expanded. The engineer who has constructed a small machine wishes to build a bigger one, the merchant who has learned how to make a little money wants to make more, the man who has been successful as a city alderman wishes to become mayor, the woman who has produced one child wants to enlarge her motherhood in another. The desire to expand one's powers moves on every level of human endeavor from that of the peddler selling his pencils on a city street to that of the general directing a military campaign.

Put in the simplest language, man wants to feel himself in action, to be secure, and to grow. He differs from the beasts, with regard to the three urges which move him, chiefly in the scope of them.[12] Man requires a much bigger area for the full movement of his faculties, and being chronically restless, he is much less likely to be contented with them. He wants to dream, to plan, to persuade, to acquire, to make—then to do all of these over again in a bigger and better way—in order to extend as far as he can the boundaries of his sensuous and dynamic existence.

In the end, the greatest difference between man and the beasts is the fact that man *thinks* about his powers. He not only is aware of how he is exercising them now, he also remembers how he exploited them yesterday (with pleasure or with pain) and he looks forward to his use of them tomorrow. He has a sense of time about his powers; it makes him reflect on them. It makes him have regrets, worries, fears, and hopes about them.

Every human being has a peculiar, inexplicably passionate feeling that he owes a kind of debt to life, a debt which he must fulfill. The leader of a nation has it, so has the beggar; it is inescapable. So man, unlike the animals, broods. He broods on the question of his adequacy in a universe of tremendous forces in which he wants to play a meaningful role. Freedom to play that role, he feels, depends upon his payment of his debt; to pay that debt he must exert himself tremendously. He must be alert, he must have energy, he must be wise and able. When he senses that he is not paying the debt as he should, he has a sense of guilt. He has "sin." The sense haunts him. It gives him "neuroses," "complexes"; it causes the murders, the suicides, the fits of anger, the deeds of desperation which we read about in newspapers and novels. It gives him also the states of depression about which we do not read.

So long as the debt to life remains, man feels that he is in a condition near to the death he fears, from which he is protoplasmically, *and so* intellectually, trying to escape. Humanly, then, the most important of man's three power urges is the impulsion to grow. Growth means a progressive movement toward the payment of one's obligation to life—away from death toward fulfillment. Man wants ever to see himself extending from yesterday into today, but more especially from today into tomorrow. Hence his peculiar affection for dawns and springtimes. In them are the promises.

From the earliest times mankind has been concerned with the rising and sinking of the life forces. These have been associated in his mind with the cycle of days. Warmth and light, he has felt, are both the source and the reflection of his own vitality; cold and darkness have a part in the ebbing of his strength. Dawn is the coming of life, twilight the receding of it. Primitive man loved the sun. It was for him the god of all things good. From it came birth, growth, healing, the power of seeing the whole world clearly and of not being afraid. The savage got up early in the morning to praise the god for his kindness, to thank him for his rising again, and to plead for his continuing blessing on man, his children, his herds, and his crops. In the primitive's mind the round of the days and man's own pattern of existence were part of a single cosmic form filled with a great longing to be ever active.

The civilized person, though he no longer chants hymns for the warmth of the sun, still feels the ebb and flow of the old forces. He feels the changing pulse beats in his family, among his friends, in the communal organism; he senses them in the receding, the decaying and the resurging, the growing of human vitality. Especially, he feels the alternations in his own nature. He notes the periods of weakness and strength, breaking and building, despairing and hoping, the general rise of his powers during the years of his youth and the fall of them in his old age. He wants mightily to live and to go on living. Those are the great passions of his existence.

Knowing, however, that in the end each must come to his death, man yearns to feel that *something* of himself—something from his body, like a son, or from his mind, like a building or a song—will have a place in the day that is coming. In that, life will continue. And, he thinks, that living part of him in the new time may be finer than what it was in the past; perhaps the son will be stronger and wiser, the building will seem taller, or the song will sound sweeter. Perhaps also the community for which he has worked will grow and prosper. Perhaps there will be more peace on earth, more understanding, more brotherly love. "Tomorrow will be better!"

The cynic doubts this. How can tomorrow be better when yesterday and today have been so bad! The fact remains, however, that hope, because inevitably it is biologically founded, is normal. It is the natural attitude of the human creature. Driven by protoplasmic compulsion, he *must* feel that there is a more vital, more effective, state of being and that striving will take him there!

II. *The Moving Seasons*

WHAT MAN FEELS about the round of the day he feels also about the seasons, for the patterns of light and warmth in both are the same. Spring is dawn; summer, noontide; autumn, twilight; and winter, night. Through the round of the seasons, like that of the day, the forces of energy flow and ebb.

In the spring life renews, in the summer it prospers, in the fall it withers, and through the long winter it lies in death. For primitive people the time of winter was one of terror. It was the period of the suspension of energies. Men were never quite sure that there would be another spring and that they would once more have the means of sustenance. They were not certain that they themselves would rise to life again. They wanted to do something about this uncertainty, so they turned to the great spirits of vegetal and animal vitality. They prayed to them; they also tried to assist them. They encouraged their gods to be active. They leapt in the fields to make the grain come up tall and strong. In order to help the gods make the ground fertile and push forth the new shoots which would produce food for men and their flocks, the people performed certain rites. They sang, danced, and pantomimed actions representing the temporary passing of life. They fasted and held sober lents. They had an act of purging in which they removed evil from the community by loading scapegoats with the forces of darkness and slaying them, or driving them away off into the mountains or the desert to die. Frequently they staged a battle between figures representing Summer and Winter—fought out so vigorously that men were actually maimed or even killed in it—then they had a festival holiday signifying the conquest of death and the rebirth of the world.

The various rites were commonly centered in one figure, a "king," selected by the community to represent it in the experience of the seasonal changes. Made to stand for something beyond and greater than his everyday self, the "king" was called upon to act out a solemn role. He was abased and "killed"—often literally—then his kingship was renewed (in himself, if alive, or in a successor, if he was not) and there was given for him a feast or "marriage" celebrating the beginning of the new fertility. The ritualistic pantomimes in which the "king" participated were accompanied by words arranged in chants and they had in them the beginnings of responsive action.[1]

It was not just the figure of life that was dramatized; always by implication there was also death. Often he was materialized. Thus life had an antagonist. In *The Golden Bough,* James Frazer tells about the appearance of this second figure in the early seasonal rites of various parts of Europe. The children used to go around with a straw-man which they took to the end of the village to burn, singing

> Now carry we Death out of the village,
> The new Summer into the village,
> Welcome, dear Summer,
> Green little corn.

On a pyre they burned the straw figure, "reviling and scoffing at it the while." Then they returned singing

We have carried away Death,
And brought Life back.
He has taken up his quarters in the village,
Therefore sing joyous songs.[2]

In time the early rituals gave birth to myths. In the myths the impersonal gods of the seasons acquired names, they became individuals and participated in events which were good for story telling. The original features of light and darkness became a little blurred; the tellers of the myth tales did not always remember the sources of their heroes. Still, the figures in essence remained the same, contestants in a struggle between life and death.

The Shinto worship of Japan looks toward the face of the sun goddess, Amaterasu-O-Mi-Kami, "Heaven Shines Great August Deity," whose principal opponent is her brother, Susano, the dark storm cloud. Fleeing from him, it is said, she once retired into a cave from which after awhile she was drawn out again by another goddess. Here, only a little disguised, are the ancient forms of Winter and Summer. Tradition tells us that Amaterasu started theatre. She leaped on a tub, thumped her heels on it and thus set a rhythm which created the fixed beat of the dramatic dance.

One of the most widely worshipped of the Middle-Eastern and Western deities was Adonis, the beautiful lord of Vegetation. Yearly he died, passing from the cheerful earth to the gloomy netherworld, and every year a divine mistress journeyed in quest of him "to the land from which there is no returning, to the house of darkness where dust lies on door and bolt." During their absence the flowers withered, the passion of love ceased to function on the earth, all of life was threatened with extinction. Women chanted a dirge for the departed Adonis using for their grief the image of a female mourner.

> Her lament is for woods, where tamarisks grow not.
> Her lament is for a wilderness where no cypresses grow.
> Her lament is for the depth of a garden of trees, where honey and wine grow not.
> Her lament is for meadows, where no plants grow.
> Her lament is for a palace, where length of life grows not.[3]

In the course of the journey below even the goddess herself was overcome, but finally the powers of the infernal region relented and Adonis and his mistress returned to the living world.

In the Greek version of the myth Adonis was a handsome youth beloved by Aphrodite. When he was a baby she hid him in a chest which she gave for safe keeping to Persephone, queen of the underworld, but when Persephone opened the chest and saw the beauty of the child she refused to give him back. Aphrodite was very angry. Zeus, assuming the role of a celestial King Solomon, settled the dispute between the goddesses of Love and Death by decreeing that Adonis should spend half the year above ground with one and half below with the other.

The counterparts of Adonis were many: Tammuz, Baal, Attis, Osiris, Heracles, Dionysus and in one form of the myth, Persephone herself, daughter of the earth Mother, Demeter.[4] Sometimes Adonis was a symbol of vegetation alone; sometimes he stood for animal life as well. In certain of his phases he partook of the nature of a powerful sun god. In all of the stories told of him, however, and in all the yearly rituals performed in his behalf, he was conceived as a great spirit of fertility which died and rose again.[5] As such he was the object of alternating lamentation and rejoicing.

From the marriage of myth and ritual came drama. Myth supplied characters and story. Ritual gave emotion and performance: responsive chanting, pantomime, and dancing. Together they produced a religious, but lifelike, re-enacting of exalted events. The first protagonists were gods, or godlike men, and only gradually was this concept humanized.

Western theatre started in the myth-and-ritualistic ceremonies of ancient Egypt. Planned for various formal occasions, they contained verse arranged to be spoken by different priests, and dealt with struggles between constructive and destructive forces. The most typical of the early ceremonies were associated with Osiris, god of the sun, life, and the human soul; his treacherous death, and his rising again. One of the ceremonials, now called the *Abydos Passion Play*, more than four thousand years old, is described by a man, Ikhernofret, who acted in it. He tells of a procession of the good god Upwawet proceeding to champion his father Osiris; a naval encounter in which the enemies of the god were overthrown; the treacherous death of Osiris at the hands of his evil brother Set; a recovery of his body, the mournful bearing of him to his tomb in Pekar; then his great resurrection, and his return to his palace amid "jubilation in the western highlands."

The tradition of the dramatic myth-rituals of Egypt passed across the Mediterranean to Greece, from it sprang the Dionysiac festivals, and from them the dramas we know. Dionysus was the god of trees, of grain, and general agriculture. He was also the personification of the vine and the exhilaration produced by the juice of the grape. The Grecian form of his name was Bacchus, or "Iacchos," derived from the wild cries of his followers. Like other gods of vegetation, Dionysus was believed to have died a violent death and then to have been brought back to life. Various stories tell how he was slain as an infant by the Titans and made alive again when his mother, Demeter, pieced his limbs together; and how Zeus swallowed his heart and begat him afresh by another mother, Semele. In the period of the year associated with his return from death, the citizens of Athens chanted choric odes on this theme. After a while some odes became partially secularized; they dealt with the passions of human heroes instead of the gods; and from these evolved the dramas of Aeschylus, Sophocles, and Euripides.[6] With the growth of the theatric forms, however, the religious spirit of springtime rites continued. The plays were still given during the festival period and were preceded by a procession in which leading citizens carried baskets filled with the first fruits of the season.

While one force in the development of Western theatre came from the myth-rituals of the Dionysiac festivals, a second sprang out of the Easter rites of the medieval church. The beginnings of liturgical drama were in the responsive passages of chanted services.[7]

Christ was the Son of God. He was also the "King" of men, who, assuming the role of a scapegoat, took upon himself the sins of men—the qualities that made them destructible—was killed, lay in a tomb for three days (representing, if one wishes, the three months of winter), and rose again. Christ was thus the glorious symbol of returning life.[8] At every anniversary of his resurrection his followers still sing a hymn called "Welcome Happy Morning!" which has as its second stanza:

> Earth her joy confesses, clothing her for spring,
> All fresh gifts returned with her returning King:
> Bloom in every meadow, leaves on every bough,
> Speak his sorrow ended, hail his triumph now.

The priests of Jesus, like the celebrants of Osiris and Dionysus, wanted to make more vivid their feelings concerning the return of their Lord, so they dramatized them. Their first expressions were in the form of "tropes," or interpolations in the Easter mass, chanted or spoken by priests who impersonated the angels and the three Marys at the tomb of Christ. In the *Concordia Regularis* of the tenth century in England, Ethelwold, Bishop of Winchester, supplied to the Benedictine monks what is in effect a brief script for drama. The bishop instructs the priests: "While the third lesson is being chanted, let four brethren vest themselves. Let one of these, vested in an alb, enter as though to take part in the service, and let him approach the sepulchre without attracting attention and sit there quietly with a palm in his hands." He is the angel. Then the other three: "Let them all, vested in copes . . . stepping delicately as those who seek something, approach the sepulchre." The angel is to say: "*Quem quaeritis in sepulchro, O Christicolae?*" (Whom seek ye in the sepulchre, O Christians?) The Marys reply: "*Ihesum Nazarenum crucifixum, O Caelicolae*" (Jesus of Nazareth the Crucified, O Heavenly One), and the angel answers: "*Non est hic; resurrexit sicut praedixerat*" (He is not here,

He is risen as He foretold). Then the three Marys turn with exultation to the choir and cry: "*Alleluia! resurrexit Dominus*" (Alleluia! the Lord is risen).[9]

The *Quem quaeritis* passage was gradually expanded until it included events before and after the sepulchre scene. More characters were added to the drama, and the action was extended to other parts of the church, then to the churchyard outside, then to the marketplace nearby. In time these religious plays, like those of Greece, became secularized; the performance of them was taken over by the trade guilds and the church cut its connection with them. From the early dramatization of the resurrection, the ascension, and the birth of Jesus came other plays about Biblical figures, some serious, like the one of Abraham and Isaac, some comic like that of Noah and his wife. The Miracles, as the more elaborate of the Biblical dramas were called, led to the Moralities, then the secular Interludes. Out of a fusion of elements from the Interludes and classical sources sprang the tragedies and comedies of Thomas Kyd, Christopher Marlowe, Robert Greene, William Shakespeare, and the other great Elizabethan playwrights.

It is significant that the classical and native strains which united to make the drama we know today originated in seasonal rites of resurrection—one of Dionysus and the other of Jesus. Both came from root ideas, or *feelings*, regarding life—a fear of death, a yearning for the full resurgence of vitality, and a joy in its return. That one source was pagan and the other Christian does not alter the fact that the two strains were alike at their core: they were in the profoundest sense biologic. A recognition of this does not destroy in any way the divine concept of the resurrections. Rather it enhances it. It integrates the godly idea with the whole process of living existence: in the glorious re-arising of the god-men Dionysus and Jesus one sees expressed the apotheosis of the god-affected protoplasmic will. Divine resurrection is Life triumphant.

From the days of the Greeks and the medieval church to our present time, theatre has evolved into various forms, few of which now bear much direct resemblance to the rituals and myths that were their ancestors. But the blood of descent is in them. Theatric art still deals with the flow and ebb of human energies—with the effort of man to reach a larger sense of organized vitality or with his sinking into a state of weakness and death. Sometimes the failure is physical, sometimes mental, sometimes spiritual; but the effect is the same. The individual who suffers failure passes for a time from the world of living men. If the nature of the ebb is final, the man enters a condition of unending winter; if it is not, he may rise again in another spring.

Beneath the upward push of man, his striving to reach a state of sunlight and summer, are the three great urges described in the preceding chapter: to exercise his powers, to preserve them, and to expand them. Some of the drama of today is concerned with the first urge only; it celebrates man's pleasure in the awareness of his faculties. It shows man using his senses, the muscles of his body, or the nerves of his brain joyously—but that is all. More of our plays now deal with man's efforts to preserve the exercise he has or to develop that exercise in new adventure. When man succeeds he feels surging through him the spirit of light; when he cannot exercise or preserve or reach out his powers he is chilled by a sense of darkness.

The long history of theatre has evolved through three stages. In the beginning there were the powerful gods who ruled the forces of heat and cold, sunlight and darkness. They were general presences and had no definite names. Theatre started when man characterized them, made myth-stories about them, and mimicked their struggles in pantomime and responsive speech. The second step was taken when the presentation of the gods gave way to the acting-out of godlike men; the third step, when the physical nobility of the early protagonists changed into a spiritual rather than a bodily eminence. The willful exercise of power by the original deities evolved gradually into a will-filled search by mortals for the quality of godliness. In all of these steps, the inward hero of the action was man, man with his compulsion to live continuously, to live well, and to grow.

Man still likes to contemplate his reaching desires and to give expression to them in works of art. Some of these take the form of music, some of painting, some of sculpture or of literature. The most potent of them all are in the theatre. Theatre deals with human urges through the most direct means of expression there is, man's own body (his face, hands, and voice, the showing and sounding forth of his yearning). The desires are imaged in such a way as to invite the spectator-auditor in effect to touch them, hear them, feel them and thus to enter into an acted-out effort to satisfy them.

The two fundamental elements of drama are still ritual and myth. Ritual is that part which deals with the rise and fall of human vitality and which presents this in the form of a ceremonial in front of a community of seers and hearers. The playhouse is a temple. Those who enact the rise and fall are prepared for their actions by being dressed differently from the watchers. They are placed on a raised platform, and they stand, walk, and talk as special persons for they are the descendants of the ancient priestly performers.

The myth part of drama is the crystallization, the visible forming, of the forces of nature originally celebrated in ritual. In myth they assume the shapes of gods and men. Spectators viewing a dramatic protagonist today may not think directly of Winter and Summer, but behind and within the heroic figure that walks and talks before them on the stage they do glimpse the spirit of Osiris, Set, Dionysus, Prometheus, Jesus, or Satan; or of one of those legendary man-figures which have acquired through imagination the souls of gods—proud Agamemnon, vengeful Clytemnestra, loyal Antigone, death-dealing Medea, tragic Oedipus, searching Faust, such a lofty struggler as Joan of Arc, or Napoleon, St. Francis of Assisi, George Washington, or Abraham Lincoln; or of a great character out of the Bible such as Joshua or David. In that large human image an audience senses again the stir of the primal powers of life and death.

Myth then is the *personalization* of ritual. It is the identification of the forces involved in rise and fall with personages—"big people"—having bodies and names. It uses traditional story forms, ancient as man himself, and fills them with special meaning. The leading figures in the stories of our time may be called "John" and "Jim," and superficially they may look like the individuals one sees on the streets or in one's home, but the audience in the theatre feels that they are more than that if their qualities are like those of the established myth men. So "John" is seen as a hero, a king, and "Jim" is seen as a king's son. Their struggles and their failures are important to those who watch, for these personages are the royal representatives of mankind.

Thus the best of theatre is still a kind of religious exercise. It leads to ecstasy. The playwright and the actor are the celebrants of man's aspiration toward a state of greater order, of a more effective organization of powers. They are leaders in the struggle from "sin," the sense of inadequacy, to "virtue," a feeling of potency, of protoplasmic fulfillment, controlled and growing.

III. *The Battle of Summer and Winter*

SUMMER *vs.* WINTER—Day *vs.* Night, Light *vs.* Darkness—this has been from the beginning the central theme of drama. Summer stands for the physical and spiritual life of man. It is warmth, it is brightness, it stimulates growth, it is growth itself; it is good. Winter represents the death of all things. It is coldness, it is dullness, it is decay; it is therefore bad.[1] Between Summer and Winter is eternal warfare. The struggle was joined in the consciousness of man when he first became a thinking being and it will continue to be of concern to him as long as he exists to deliberate, feel, plan, and act on the opposing forces which affect his welfare.

In early times the Sun, god of Summer, was conceived as a fighter. He was obliged to strangle the serpents of the Night and battle with great clouds and fierce storms. When daily he sank below the western horizon he had to struggle for several hours with the restraining waters beneath the earth before he could rise again in the east. The greatest of his wrestlings were of course the long and mighty ones with the seasonal powers which tried to hold him. They affected him deeply; when he was angry at them he blazed forth, when he was sulky he hid himself, when he was happy, as he was apt to be in the time of springtide victory, he leapt joyfully. There is an old tradition in Europe that the sun dances three times on

Easter morning.[2] The resurrection of Jesus, the hope of mankind, is celebrated with a solar joy because the God-Man himself is the "light of the world."[3]

Men have long recognized the primal conflict between the forces of warmth and light on one side and those of chill and darkness on the other, and they have tried to give their own strength to aid the forces of summer. They have done this, as we have noted, in vigorous rituals of action. In ceremonials of ancient Crete groups of "fair men" fought "black men." In various parts of Europe "summer bands" engaged "winter bands" in contest. In Egypt attacking warriors representing the evil god, Set, held very realistic battles with a company of defenders which guarded the precious body of the sun-god, Osiris. Often the great Pharoah stepped in at the end of conflict—in which the company of Osiris always contrived to win—in order that the most shining one present might impersonate the force of resurrection now triumphant.

The first conflicts in every country were quite physical since primitive people are not much given to abstractions. Later the warfare between Summer and Winter became more representational. Whether or not the figures of Life and Death still opposed each other in bodily form they were presumed to be there in spirit. Seldom now does the protagonist, the exponent of some special aspect of Summer, engage in a visible struggle with Winter, but his mind and his heart oppose it. Even the most intellectual of today's encounters are fundamentally belligerent affairs; what is argued over, *battled* over, is always related to a human concern about the potency, the adequacy, of human living. In ancient times the adherent of Osiris was a shepherd or a tiller of the soil who helped to wrestle with the power of Set so that he, the man, might have health, that his flocks and crops might increase, and that his family might grow in numbers and in strength. Now the champion of Summer is a man of enterprise, a person of principle, a leader of moral forces, an individual working on the side of greater energy, brilliance, uprightness, or vision who struggles with powers of weakness, dullness, corruption, or blindness with the purpose of winning over them. Those who watch the conflict feel themselves in it; their kindred urges are stirred and they themselves become emotionally involved in the outcome of the contest they are following.

Romeo and Juliet are proponents of the force of Summer. The heat of their love battles with the coldness of the hatred between their families. Hamlet is a prince of Light who struggles with the Darkness of his uncle and his nightmarish court. The Emperor Jones is a king of Courage (an aspect of the Summer quality) who pits his strength against the Formless Fears in the forest. Nora Helmer is Vision (allied to the forces of Light) who, in spite of her frailties, fights valiantly and wins against the Blindness of her husband. Sometimes Summer (or Light, or Courage, or Vision) wins; sometimes it loses. Whatever the names of the opponents the essential battle is the same, and for the spectator it is always exciting and important.

The materials of drama, old or new, are a man and his environment. At the center is the intimate spark, the core of human powers, which the man regards as "himself." It is his soul. It is this spark in each that make Romeo and Juliet the lovers they are. It is this spark in Hamlet that drives him to speak to his father's ghost, then after the interview to struggle for his father's honor. It is this spark which Hamlet (in all his roles) addresses in his soliloquies.

The personal spark is always attached to Summer. It is so attached even when the human creature in which it burns seeks not his growth but his self destruction, for the leap to death is never conceived in drama as being dark and quiet but illuminated and vigorous. The act of this kind of dying gathers to itself a kind of glory, like the sudden blaze of an ember before it is extinguished.[4] So the soul of man, taking to itself for the period of its existence the quality of Summer, of Daytime, of Light, for which it yearns, must ever be seen as "good." Its goodness may not be glimpsed by other humans unable to penetrate to the inward glow, but to the man who owns the spark—whose essence, whose soul, is the spark—that spark is good. It is the greatest good that there is for him.

Moving around the spark of Summer are various forces with which the man must reckon. Some are beneficial, capable of intensifying the spark; some are harmful, threatening to extinguish it. In so far as they help or hinder the glowing core of the man to feel the exercise, preservation, or extension of his powers the environmental influences belong to the grand categories of Summer or of Winter. Both the good and the bad forces are found in objects of nature such as snow and rain, the forest around one's home, or the cutworms in one's garden. Many others, as already noted, are in the attitude of one's family, one's neighbors, the people with whom one works. Some of the Summer and Winter environmental forces—those which are finally the strongest and most effective—are within the man's own nature. They are in the "other parts" of the personality which surround the spark of the man: his physical strength, his liking for music, his ability to organize people, his unfortunate appetite for liquor, his fear of ridicule. Hamlet has charm; Hamlet has intelligence; he also has sensitivity, doubts of his own adequacy in a course of action. The Emperor Jones is both courageous and fearful. Nora Helmer has love, understanding, and courage; she also has some feminine weaknesses which make it difficult for her to exert the best of her powers. So the battle of Summer and Winter is fought inside as well as outside.

There can be no Warmth without Cold, no Light without Darkness. They have a meaning only in contrast. The Sun of Egypt which sank lazily in the west had to purge the qualities of indolence it picked up during its daytime journey by washing itself in the chilly waters under the earth. It had to wrestle with the forces of Night to regain its strength and prepare itself for its brave new rise in the east. Summer needs Winter to evoke its power. This kind of need exists as truly in the animal world as it does in the physical. Biologists have observed how the growth and renewal of species depends on struggle. Serial cultures of unicellular organisms cared for under the best of temperature and feeding conditions invariably lose their vitality and die. The same is true of fruit flies. Flocks of sea gulls near St. Augustine, Florida, were fed for years from the scraps thrown to them from the shrimp fleets around which they hovered. When the fleets moved to Key West, the gulls starved, not because there was any lack of fish along the beaches, but because the gulls had lost the knack of catching them. Struggle means life; ease means death.[5]

The necessity for continuous challenge exists in the human being, both singly and in groups. Note how the popular idol in high school (like the Gentleman Caller in Williams's *The Glass Menagerie*) becomes so often a failure in adult life. Arnold Toynbee has commented on the fact that healthy societies are produced by difficult rather than easy circumstances. The vigorous, active groups of people have always achieved eminence only after conflict; and if later, following success, they drift too long without having to exert themselves against contrary groups, they usually sink, like the Protozoa and the sea gulls, into a state of decay. Fighting and growing seem to belong together.

Human beings by their very nature as protoplasmic substances sense the importance of struggle. Since it is necessary for their welfare they are excited about it. Our newspapers, magazines, histories, and novels are much more occupied with hazardous undertakings, conquests and defeats, with strong disagreements and conflicts between divergent personalities than they are with subjects of peace. Challenge alerts the organism. It awakens the senses; it makes the heart beat quickly; it induces the muscles to tense, to be ready for action. How pleasant to the warrior his posture may be before battle is suggested in the charge Shakespeare has the king in *Henry V* make to his soldiers at Harfleur:

In peace there's nothing so becomes a man
As modest stillness and humility;
But when the blast of war blows in our ears,
Then imitate the action of the tiger;
Stiffen the sinews, summon up the blood,

Disguise fair nature with hard-favour'd rage;
Then lend the eye a terrible aspect;

. . . .

Now set the teeth and stretch the nostril wide,
Hold hard the breath, and bend up every spirit
To his full height. On, on, you noblest English!

King Henry closes his speech with an expression of desire, in which all presumably share, for the battle to begin:

I see you stand like greyhounds in the slips,
Straining upon the start. The game's afoot!
Follow your spirit!

Countless human records are filled with the wail of pain caused by the suffering which accompanies conflict. Yet sounding with that cry is usually, strangely, a sometimes muffled but quite persistent song of pleasure. Struggle for the victory of Summer is good and the hope that goes with it is sweet. Since the desire for betterment, the hope that it may be achieved and the fighting that is required have become so inextricably united in human feeling, the fighting itself has acquired a value sometimes quite unconnected with any clear goal for it. Colonel Theodore O'Hara, in his famous old poem, "The Bivouac of the Dead," refers to the "fierce delight" and the "rapture" of conflict. He writes about a sensuous pleasure. On a different level of contemplation, Maxwell Anderson sings in *Winterset* of the ecstasy, perhaps bitter but still very real, of those who go on fighting with their spirits even when they are not sure just what there is out in the great universe to fight for.

On this star,
in this hard star-adventure, knowing not
what the fires mean to right and left, nor whether
a meaning was intended or presumed,
man can stand up, and look out blind, and say:
in all these turning lights I find no clue,
only a masterless night, and in my blood
no certain answer, yet is my mind my own,
yet is my heart a cry toward something dim
in distance, which is higher than I am
and makes me emperor of the endless dark
even in seeking!

The playwright sees this attitude as good.

Man's fighting instinct is inherent and strong; it has a long ancestry. One can observe the trait on every step of the ladder of evolution, from the bottom to the top.[6] In man, among all the animals, the warrior trait is most persistent because it is engaged with mental factors which do not complicate the attitudes of beasts. One of the most potent is tradition. From time immemorial the warrior has held an enviable position at the top of the community. He has been headman, law-giver, and king, admired by the men and beloved by the women. In primitive days man had to fight to survive. In later days he fought for honor—in his mind, a Summer value. In many instances he was merely looking for an excuse to fight.

Today we still admire the "scrapper," the man who, beginning conflict, has the hardihood to "stay with it" and does not run away. Often, the thing which keeps a man struggling against an adversary, long after he knows the uselessness of the effort and his friends are not around to encourage him, is just his stubborn pride in his quality as a fighter.

Fundamentally the attitude of the struggler has goodness in it, one might say, not because his posture in itself has virtue, but because the posture *implies beyond* a better condition to which the human organism aspires. The goal may not even be completely clear—and from another individual's viewpoint it may seem not to be worthy at all—but a man's willingness to fight, at least, means that protoplasmic impulses are pushing the human creature toward new adjustments with surrounding facts. So long as a man is struggling he is biologically and spiritually alive.

If it is true that struggling itself has acquired a great, sometimes fearsome, sometimes glorious, meaning, that meaning is ultimately limited. *Finally there must be a quality of Summer to fight for.* Summer, in the end, is what all the acting, all the thinking, all the writing, all the talking is about. Perhaps for short periods a man may be occupied with fighting alone; he may get pleasure out of just the sense of having his physical and mental faculties put into violent motion—for their own sake. But that is not growth. In the long run there must be a goal related to an idea of betterment, and there must be a hope that the goal can be reached.

For an individual the good goal, the Summer goal, is that which has in it the force of total integration, the experiencing of the fact of living richly and fully. In temporal man the quality of the Summer goal is an effective organization of physical and mental powers. In religious man the quality is "godliness." The essence of both is the same.

The quality of Winter which a person tries to escape is the reverse of this. It is frustration, confusion, inadequacy. It may be an active destructiveness. In biological man it is disintegration. In religious man it is "evil." Again, the essence is the same.

There are two ways in which a man may strive to achieve the values of Summer. One is by fighting and dispelling the elements of Winter which threaten his progress. That has already been considered. The other way is by attaching himself to some other person or some other object which already has in it an element of the Summer he desires. For Romeo, Juliet is Summer; he wants to be near her, united with her goodness. Without her he feels he is in a state of Winter—an incomplete and therefore discontented man. When in the tomb he thinks she is dead, he drinks the vial of poison believing that through his own physical death—this bit of physical Winter—he will be able to reach beyond to a spiritual Summer with his beloved.

Plays concerning the course of affection between men and women offer the clearest and most common examples of the drama of attachment. The union they deal with is related to the furtherance of life. Boy sees in girl, or girl sees in boy, the means to a Summer of happiness and he or she is ready and eager to struggle for what the union promises. And so every dramatist who deals with the theme of love is almost bound to set up for his composition the same old formula: "Boy meets girl. . . . Boy wants girl. . . . Boy loses girl. . . . Boy gets girl!"

But after the marriage the climate of the seasons may change. The Summer of union may turn out to be incomplete; the boy and the girl may now long for a child, or for a better home, or for a place in society in which their best powers can express themselves *more* freely. So now there will be a struggle for a larger Summer.

Or maybe the marriage turns out not to be a Summer at all, and one or both of the principals begin to look elsewhere for a "*real* one." Jason, wedded to Medea, longs for Creusa. Craig's wife, in the modern play by George Kelly, tries to find her happiness in the decorations of her house. Sometimes the new Summer appears to exist in books, in writing, in travel (an experience of far-away places), in work with people who seem to have more friendliness, more understanding, and helpfulness than one's mate. So the reaching for attachment moves on.

The quality of Summer to which a protagonist reaches does not, of course, have to have any relation to marriage at all. Macbeth wants a crown. In kingship he feels he will have an exercise for his peculiar personal powers which he could enjoy in no other state. Yank, in *The Hairy Ape*, longs for the association of other men, he wants to "belong," because he thinks their words and their action will reveal to him the kind of man he really is and thus give him a release from the doubts that haunt him. In *Desire Under the Elms*, Abbie reaches for a farm. That stands for her as a Summer of security. But when she comes close enough to grasp the farm, she sees that there is something else she wants even more than security; and it is about this second thing that the principal part of the drama revolves.

Attachments may mean the acquisition of new powers; or attachments may mean a way for the preservation or the release of powers which now exist but have not so far been able fully to exert themselves. So the very act of association—like the act of conflict—has grown up in Nature to have a significance of its own. Nature wants plants and animals to cling together so that they can help each other be productive. Because man, as a part of the world of nature, senses the importance of association, he has made virtues out of kindliness, loyalty, consideration, and attitudes of protectiveness toward weaker members of his family and his social group.

To state, as some philosophers do, that the aggressive, competitive element marks the biggest part of man's character is to view him narrowly. The first law of the animal world—and man is not excepted in this—is not competition but *cooperation*. It is true that animal nature strives to advance itself, but it is true also that it strives to advance others, for in that advance the individual shares. Says the eminent zoologist, Robert Coker, a living creature "tends to grow and to multiply, not for itself alone, but for the promotion and increase of its kind, even though for the production of its kind it must [sometimes] sacrifice some part or the whole of itself. . . . The worker bees that give up all capacity for self-propagation to spend their entire lives in the protection, feeding and nursing of the larvae and of the queen, the one reproductive member of the colony; the drone bee that sacrifices his life in the mating process . . . and the seed that sprouts and so hastens the end of its own individual existence; the man that lays down his life for country or principle—these are all obeying the same law of nature."[7]

This inclination to be cooperative is evident on all levels of life. In his little book, *On Being Human*, the anthropologist Ashley Montagu describes certain laboratory experiments that demonstrated this. The cells of a frog's egg during an early state of its development were shaken apart and placed in water some distance from one another. The separated cells slowly approached each other until they were united again. Individual bacteria joined to form a common nonreproductive stalk at the top of which only were cyst-like forms which did the propagating. Caterpillars, set apart from each other, sought out the company of their fellows, and even their isolated larvae tended to seek their kind.[8]

This "social appetite," as Montagu calls it, which motivates the lesser beasts operates on all the higher steps of evolution. It is seen in the flocking of birds, the herding of deer, and the community labor of such workers as the beavers. Animals living together survive better, recover from their wounds more quickly, and grow more rapidly. It seems as if the very presence of others of their kind intensifies for them the whole process of existence and expansion.[9]

Montagu points out the fact that the solitary animal is rare. Throughout, natural selection favors the social creatures. It is significant that few isolated persons are to be found in the history of humanity. Civilization has been able to evolve only through the efforts of those mindful of the community. Commerce, industry, legislation, education, literature, and art, which give the measure of man's development through the ages, are all activities which require a consistent interaction between the individual and the group. Even those persons who have gone out to subjugate other societies have invariably done so in the name of their own tribes or nations.

While man *fights*, he *loves something*, something which has to do with Summer. The love is the cause of the fighting. If we accept the notion that men enjoy combat and do not need to be urged into it, we must acknowledge also that there would not be much persistence about it if there were not something to fight for. The Summer element which a man seeks may have a frankly social aspect: the safety or integrity of a whole community or the security of a family. Or it may seem to be something quite personal, like the man's possessions, or his ambitions, or his honor. The interesting fact about the "personal" objects, however, is that essentially they are connected with one's relationship to others. A man fights for his possessions *in order* to be able to provide well for his family. He fights for the achievement of an ambition *in order* to impress a woman or the intimate friends on whose good will his feeling of well-being depends. He fights for his honor *in order* to maintain his sense of acceptability in the group. Ever in his mind is the haunting fear of social incompetence. As the circle turns in this universe of interrelatedness social incompetence means personal failure, and personal failure means that one's powers make no mark. With no mark there is no assurance that one is moving toward a Summer beyond. In essence the man who fails to exert himself effectively for others ceases to be effective to himself; spiritually he is dead.

Since being loved makes for a feeling of warm security, of being in the swim of life, man desires love tremendously. Love, says Montagu, "is what the human being seeks all his life, and society, culture, and man's institutions, however inefficient some of them may be, all exist to secure that one fundamental satisfaction. The emotional need for love is as definite and compelling as the need for food."[10] It is true that all of us are acquainted with certain men who seem to possess no quality of affection in any part of them. They appear to be men of hatred only. Often on closer acquaintance, however, one finds that the bitterness they show is only a mask for disappointment. They are hurt and indignant because their natural powers of love have no outlet. By inclination they are lovers. Observe the heroes in Strindberg's plays. Behind their barriers their hatred is painful to them and they would like to rid themselves of it if they could. Such men make very good drama. Deep in the heart of each is an ideal which he cherishes. This he will do battle for when occasion offers. If the ideal is strong and the hurt regarding it is keen enough, the battle will be vigorous.

What is undramatic is the bitterness to which no contrary love is attached. That is the kind which comes out of weakness. Its quality is ugly. It has no beauty because it starts with no passion and it leads to no combat. The character in a play which is pervaded by such an emotion is without a spiritual muscle; in the pattern of the revolving seasons he is a drifter only, crying noisily for a lazy death. The rebirth of Spring and the upward struggle into Summer hold little appeal for him; he lacks the strength to make himself a part of them. Love is always associated with growth. Without love there cannot be motion; and without that motion there cannot be drama.

Dramatic art then is a celebration of both human conflict and human affection. The two are inseparable. Combat is exciting; the fighter is an exhilarated person. But a work of drama is incomplete without the lover. Every protagonist must have a passion for belonging—to an idea, to a person, or to a group. Back of the desire for union is a concept of well-being longed for, to be struggled for.

At the beginning of *Hamlet* the Prince is in no personal danger; he is well cared for, properly honored, and has all the freedom he could desire. Yet he decides to fight. For what? To avenge his father's death. What motivates his struggle throughout is his sense of loyalty to the best elements—the honor, the integrity—of his family and his desire to see that the essence of this be preserved. It is important to him as a person; without it his mental powers of reasoning and his spiritual sense of order are stifled. Without the freeing of the soul of his family he himself cannot feel free. He achieves his spiritual desire though his body dies.

Nora in *A Doll's House* is a pampered woman. She has financial security, a comfortable home, two healthy children, and an indulgent husband. Yet she decides to struggle. For what? To put a foundation under her self-respect. She sees her position, not only in her family, but also in society; she wants to be able to hold her head up in the community and be regarded as a complete individual —the kind of person that gives to the community its basic vitality and so makes her have a reason for living. Regina's conflict in *The Little Foxes* likewise is related to union. Her motives are thoroughly selfish, but a thought for society is strong in them. She is profoundly concerned about the opinion of her acquaintances; she wants to be admired by them for her wealth, envied by them for her position. Though her love for the group is an inverted one it is nevertheless active. What she gets in the end, a sense of fear, has its significance in the prospective attitude of those very persons she has struggled to impress. Unlike Nora, she arrives at a feeling that she has lost power. Instead of being free to grow, she has blighted herself and will eventually die.

The most powerful factor giving direction to a dramatic conflict is often the sense of a union growing, not at the end of fighting, but during the course of it. While the protagonist is struggling he is consciously or unconsciously driving himself to a new, closer, and more productive relationship with the physical world, the human world, or some creative force of the spiritual world. Perhaps he is a farmer's boy hating the soil while he dreams of another life in a far-away city. He fights the ground, wrestling with its grip on his muscles and his rebellious mind, only to find in the end that it is not his enemy but his friend. Perhaps the fighter is a woman, bound by social conventions to a humiliating position in the community. She struggles with the conventions and works out for herself a new and better relation with the very powers which have pressed upon her. Or perhaps a man has feared a weakness in himself—his conscience or his sensitivity. He fights that trait of himself and reshapes the weakness into a strength, thereby achieving a feeling of peace with himself (that part which is in tune with the light-filled, creative force of the Universe). In a work of dramatic art, the warrior gets at the close of his battle a new stability. Sometimes it is on the level toward which he has labored, sometimes it is on quite a different level; but an adjustment has been achieved. The spectator, sympathetically following the course of the conflict and the final union, feels himself likewise stabilized.

A working attitude toward the problems of the theatre which has long been regarded as standard is the one based on the famous statement by the French critic, Ferdinand Brunetière: "The theatre in general is nothing but the place for the development of the human will, attacking the obstacles opposed to it by destiny, fortune or circumstances." With it goes another statement. "Drama is a representation of the will of man in conflict with the mysterious powers or natural forces which limit and belittle us [the passionate essence of us]; it is one of us thrown living upon the stage, there to struggle against fatality, against social law, against one of his fellow-mortals, against himself, if need be, against the ambitions, the interests, the prejudices, the folly, the malevolence of those who surround him." William Archer in *Play-Making* attacked this concept of drama, pointing out that while it serves most plays it does not apply to all. Among those compositions which he thinks have no major conflicts—and so no significant acts of will—are *Oedipus*, *Othello*, and *Ghosts*.

Archer's argument, taken as a whole, is rather logical. One wonders, however, if he did not fail to take into account two things which support Brunetière. It is true that Oedipus, Othello, and Mrs. Alving do not—cannot—put up any very direct fight against the forces that press against them, but the fact that they will not easily accept them, that they writhe resistantly under their push—in effect press back against the opposing forces, perhaps blindly but strongly—suggests a kind of struggle. Then there is the participating observer; he plays an important role in drama and must not be ignored. In the Greek theatre a part of the drama frequently passed from the principal actors to the chorus, which was a kind of representative of the spectators. It spoke the thoughts of the audience and gave expression to its fears and its wishes. Often it gave sympathetic advice to the protagonist, warning him of evil and suggesting a way to avoid it. Sometimes it spoke of its love and regard for this man. When the blind Tiresias tells Oedipus that he is his own curse, the chorus chants in defense of its king:

> Never . . . by the verdict of my heart shall he be adjudged guilty of crime.

When Jocasta, knowing at last the dark secret of the king's birth, rushes troubled back into the palace, the chorus prays for its troubled lord:

> If I am seer or wise of heart, O Cithaeron, thou shalt not fail—by yon heaven, thou shalt not!—to know at tomorrow's full moon that Oedipus honours thee as native to him, as his nurse, and his mother, and that thou are celebrated in our dance and song, because thou art well-pleasing to our prince. O Phoebus to whom we cry, may these things find favour in thy sight![11]

Thus the chorus was anything but neutral. In this play, as in *Agamemnon*, *Antigone*, and the other downward-moving tragedies, the choral body, while it never fought the destroying forces physically, wrestled with them spiritually, and so gave the speechless audience the feeling that vicariously it was aiding the conflict on behalf of the hero whose own powers to fight back were limited by his circumstances. In later plays, both the Elizabethan and modern, the chorus was eliminated, but the audience's participation continued. The villain, Iago, and the ghosts of Mrs. Alving's house do have strong opponents; a part of them, at least, are not in visible costume but in the minds of the spectators.

One gets the best answer to Archer's question, however, when one takes a broader view of the plays than the one the critic permitted himself. If one looks at the dramas in the light of their seasonal aspects one sees at once that each has a big, clear conflict, centered in individuals, but not in individuals who are meeting each other head-on in one thin line. In the plays described, the protagonist and antagonist are each representative of a whole group of forces, one constructive (having the quality of Summer) and one destructive (with the spirit of Winter). Throughout the play of *Oedipus* the larger issue is not the king's happiness but the state's health. He struggles to save that and Thebes becomes free. When Oedipus suffers agony he does so in the role of the community's scapegoat. He is the part of Thebes that must be purged, even if the purging means pain to its king.

In much of *Othello* the envious Iago opposes his general on a broad front, and only when this has failed does he attack the Moor's strength on a personal detail, his love for Desdemona. Othello's jealousy is his Achilles' heel, not the whole man which represents the sweep of the Summertime forces. The dark Iago is trying to resist the whole. Othello, as a general, fights back against the total disorderliness of which Iago happens to be the most active unit. *Ghosts* likewise is a drama of wide opposition; it is not just a piece of pointed combat. Mrs. Alving is fighting with the ghosts of the house taken as a big group of resisting devils. They are the Darkness; they are the Winter.

Mrs. Alving stands for the Light. Her forces fail. In their sinking she becomes a tragic figure.[12]

So in general Brunetière's statement seems still to be a good one. A story drawn around a character who is unchallenged is bound to be static. If he moves at all he will go in a straight line, and then with only little force. If, however, he has to *fight* for something, something he cherishes, he will move vigorously—thrusting, parrying, dodging, thrusting again.[13] As he does this he will reveal interestingly the various facets of himself and compel conditions about him to change continuously with him. That is worth watching!

Theatre, we have said, is related to the seasons. Different segments of human life have in them the nature of Springtime, Summer, and Fall. Winter is the time of the human career that poets and dramatists treat as being inimical to man's spirit. No single individual can avoid it. However, a group of persons can. In a community of people there are births as well as deaths, life rising as well as life sinking; so the essential vitality does in effect go on. In the group there is continuity; in it the seasons move through their orbit.

The smallest unit in which the cycle can have completeness is the family. In it the various energies associated with human existence have their surges and recessions, their pressings upward and their slippings downward, without a break. All the elements of the family are interdependent. This accounts for the powerful feeling of attachment the various members have for each other.

Man's sociological nature has its origin in the infant's relationship with its parents. The baby lies for a time in its mother's womb. When it is born it feels, and continues to feel for some years, its dependence on its mother. Gradually it becomes conscious also of its need for the attention of its father, then of its brothers and sisters. On their good will stands the condition of the child's welfare. For related reasons the family's feeling of well-being depends on the responsiveness of the child. The mother measures her womanly powers, the father his manly powers and the brothers and sisters their several adolescent powers by the behavior of the little one. All members of the group look to each other and from that attitude grows the love they have for each other. Affection wants approval. The loving members of the family try to adapt their actions, make them helpful and pleasing, so that the good conditions will continue. Thus grows cooperative action. Anthropologists have long viewed the family group as the living cell of the citizen group. Family feeling develops into a tribal feeling, and that evolves into a regional and then a national cohesiveness. At the center of it all is the baby and its mother.

If the family is the breeding place for affections, it is likewise the home of hatreds. In a unit so tightly bound together tensions are bound to form. Sons become envious of their fathers, daughters rebel against their mothers, brothers and sisters develop fierce jealousies. These cause battles, some of which lead to intense suffering. Thus family actions illustrate most directly—often most violently—the battle of Summer and Winter.

It is significant that the family has served the theatre from time immemorial as a principal subject of drama. Shakespeare, Molière, Strindberg, Chekhov, Shaw, Synge, Molnar, Anderson, Wilder, Pirandello, and a host of other authors deal with the family. Most of the classics as well as the compositions of such present-day writers as Ibsen, O'Neill, Miller, and Williams are so centered. In nearly all of these plays is very strong action; in many there is even murder or suicide. In the heart of every play, however, is a passionate affection. That is the premise, the starting point. The affection wishes to be fulfilled; it supplies a drive for all that is done.

The themes of these dramas can be easily diagrammed with reference to their opposing qualities seen in the light of the three fundamental urges of man:

Related to the Urge to Exercise Powers
(to use one's capacities)

Sensuous Enjoyment	[Dullness]

Related to the Urge to Preserve, and to Enlarge, Powers

Love	Hatred
Loyalty	Disloyalty (treachery)
Courage	Cowardice

Seven of these themes are used in the theatre. The opponent of Sensuous Enjoyment—Dullness—is the one that has no value whatsoever since its essential nature denies the whole idea of theatric effect. Drama *must have stimulation*, either of Summer or of Winter; without this it cannot exist at all.

The great terror of mankind is what comes finally from a sense of disintegration. Disintegration means uselessness, having no good reason for existing in a universe of growing powers. Related to this weakness is the feeling of loneliness. Both imply inadequacy, a lack of the *stuff of life*. The only cure for them is a stronger union with a light-giving, life-giving force, one which leads to creativity, the growth and expansion of the powers man exists to use. In its final analysis then, theatre is built on the idea of cherished things, on love—on love for an object or quality of Summer, so intense that it is worth doing battle for.

IV. *King, Scapegoat, and King's Son*

WE DO NOT KNOW now whether the religious plays of ancient Egypt were all serious or if there were among them perhaps some composed and enacted in a lighter mood. There are no records of comedy. Nevertheless, the tradition of springtime festival which the Egyptians passed on to the Greeks was filled with exuberance. The Athenian drama, growing as it did out of the rites which celebrated the yearly rise of Summertime forces, was both rich and passionate. Some of it was tragic and some was comic. Greek comedy was extravertive. It was certainly active and probably noisy; it expressed frankly the kind of emotions which spring from the young part of the year. So that there might be no mistake about his relation to the seasonal rites of fertility which gave cause for his performance, each comic actor wore the symbol of the phallus.

Today we still have much theatre filled with the spirit of joyous youthfulness. Notable examples are our romantic musicals like *Oklahoma!*, our "screwball" extravaganzas like *Hellzapoppin,* and our verbal farces like *Born Yesterday*. There is nothing restrained about them, and no one needs to point out that in them the themes of wine and sex are still popular. Viewed in this aspect modern comedy is the most direct descendent of the old Dionysiac tradition we have. Looked at in a different way, however, the directness is a little blurred. No longer now does pure comedy have much to do with the reverent attitude which affected the Greeks when they came to the theatre. Comic writing tends increasingly to take two forms, one diversional and the other didactic, neither of them essentially religious. Through the ages much of the early seasonal, biologically-based attitude has given way to intellectuality so that now comedy seems to represent not so much a primary action as a commentary on it. This has worked to inhibit the flow of direct impulses and to substitute for them a contemplative, critical view of life.

In the plays modeled on the Restoration comedy of manners, for example, the subject is love; but not by any stretch of thought can this treatment of that subject be related to the concept of springtime fertility. The Restoration viewpoint, therefore, is not spiritual but witty—brainy. Wilde deals with motherhood in *The Importance of Being Earnest*, but he makes fun of it. Noel Coward's protagonists in *Private Lives* are outwardly emotional but inwardly quite cool. Shaw contemplates evolution in *Back to Methuselah*, and the life force in *Man and Superman*, but chiefly for the purpose of drawing lighthearted philosophical conclusions about them. In *Candida* he does combine an earth-rooted feeling with his mental detachment, but in such pieces as *A Doctor's Dilemma* he is principally intellectual.

There is one way, it is true, in which all effective modern comedy, even the most commentarial, is still bound to the original seasonal pattern of drama. It *takes sides*. It has a "good" force (representing, at least distantly, Summer) and a "bad" force (suggestive of Winter), and these are set in opposition to each other. Often the issue struggled over is comparatively so trivial that the spectator cannot see in it very much distinction between good and evil; he really does not care very much and finds himself interested in the battle of minds, more for itself than for anything else. The fact does remain, however, that the effect of purely mental contests tends in time to become spiritless if there is not in them at least *something worthy of emotion*, something that the audience feels it wants to have win before the evening is over. And the thing that triumphs must matter inwardly.

If to some extent the comic tradition has wandered from the main path of seasonal conflict, the more serious kinds of drama have stuck to it. This is because tragedy is basically a *feeling* drama, and the theatre of emotions is bound by its biological inheritance to be a place where the fundamental struggles of life are dealt with. Generally the hero of serious drama is set up as a man to be cherished. Since the spectator is drawn toward an attachment to him (the hero embodies certain of the good qualities which the spectator sees in himself and wants to have grow and succeed) he must fight over something important. The spectator could not tolerate having this figure struggle lightly with a few witty shafts. The hero must show strong qualities as a warrior, and he must have a fair chance to win.

Evidence points to the conclusion that the primitive springtime ceremonials in Greece from which tragedy developed honored more than just the resurrection of Dionysus. Blended with the concept of the cyclic death and rebirth of the world of nature was the idea of the rebirth of the tribe through the return of its heroes.[1] Thus the two images of drama, one derived from ritual and the other from myth, were united. Some of the sense of this composite image persists in the person of the tragic protagonist today. He is representatively human, but he is not just an ordinary individual. He is, in his way, "big." Endowed with a deep desire, a desire which has at its core something to do with an exercise, preservation, or extension of good powers, he has for the spectator, physically or spiritually (commonly both), the nature of a King.

The King has a blemish, a "tragic flaw." The fault is one which in essence is likely to appear in any man, such as cowardice, anger, greed, false pride or, very often, just a social inadequacy. He was born on the wrong side of the tracks, perhaps; he lacks strength to overcome his obstacles; he cannot understand his wife; he is too easily suspicious of his neighbor; or he cannot communicate with others freely. At heart the protagonist is a worthy man, but a weakness in his condition keeps his productive forces from operating effectively. In the organized system of an ever-creative universe, therefore, the protagonist is not "pulling his part" and his trait of inadequacy must be viewed as an evil. With his good qualities, marred by his blemish, the hero is a symbol of mankind, yearning, hoping, struggling against the forces of darkness. The King, bearing the flaw in his person, assumes the dramatic role of Scapegoat. He suffers—in classic drama he dies—causing a purging of evil.

The communal group of whom the hero takes the purge is, for the purposes of the usual story, the family, the tribe, the city, the band, or any other social unit of which he is a member. Oedipus is the king and scapegoat of Thebes. Hamlet is the prince and purge-taker of Elsinore. Yank of *The Hairy Ape* is the "strong guy" and sufferer among the nether laborers in the modern world of steam engines. Willie Loman is both head-man and low-man for the salesmen in our society.

By implication the protagonist serves more than what he seems to stand for in the play script. He represents beyond the stage the whole body of spectators, the communal celebrants in the temple of the theatre, men and women who, in watching the hero's actions, are vicariously putting their own minds and feelings into them. From the audience the figure on the stage draws a sympathetic sense of its own guilt and dread and, by burning this out in his pain, releases that body of people from its feeling of suffering.

In the play the royal scapegoat takes into himself the sickness of the dramatic group he represents. Oedipus, as stated, must purge Thebes. But his personal flaw does not correspond exactly to the evil that exists in the community. There doubtless are many angry men in that city, but a condition of anger is not the principal weakness of that place. The tragedy lies in the fact that the king, called on to help his city, finds that his flaw prevents him from doing this without a sacrifice of himself. Hamlet must destroy the corruption of his uncle and his court in order to restore the honor of his father. What the court suffers from, however, is not an excess of sensitivity—rather the opposite—but Hamlet's own sensitivity prevents him from completing his work without a painful experience on his part. In each case the personal flaw in the scapegoat helps to challenge and so to stimulate the act of atonement. Oedipus' passionate nature leads to his blinding of himself and his exile from Thebes, while Hamlet's timidity reverses itself into the violent movements which cause his death.

The seasonal ritual has four great steps. First is the recognition of the King. Then there is a death. The third step is a struggle between the forces of Summer and Winter for the soul of the King. In our drama the second and third steps are combined, giving the King himself an opportunity to enter the contest, using his Summertime forces (the flawless side of him) as the principal positive power in the battle. The fourth, the final, step is the resurrection. After the fight, the soul of the King arises. It is reborn in his own person, or in the new person of his son.

When it is developed fully, dramatic tragedy progresses definitely through this last step.[2] Hamlet in dying creates, and when he has passed leaves behind him, an image of princeliness which will, we feel, affect the community of Elsinore for a long time to come. Macbeth has always wanted to be a great monarch. The full measure of this desire is never realized in the brief course of his miserable reign, but it is in his magnificent departure from the reign. The fulfillment of the love of Romeo and Juliet rises out of their entombment. Hereafter their union will be eternal, unassailable, complete.

Occasionally the fair figure which rises from the ashes of the Old King of the year is not a doer but an undoer. He is the good part of the King, that part which senses most keenly the King's responsibility to the universal order, acting to destroy the bad part. The diseased part of Oedipus affects the city which he governs. His grandeur as king exists in his behavior as judge and nullifier of the evil which is bringing misery to his city. Oedipus the evil-maker dies, but the spirit of Oedipus the driver-out of evil rises in his place. In the modern play of *Hedda Gabler* a passionate but frustrated woman comes to realize that she is throwing the lives of all around her into disorder. She achieves a nobility, not by suddenly doing something creative—she knows she is sterile—but by clearing the community once and for all of her death-making presence. She does not creep into a pitiful oblivion. She annihilates herself with one clean gesture. Now the grateful community will have some respect for her memory.

The full course of the resurrection is seen most clearly in those tragedies which provide a glimpse of the coming of a King's Son. Often his image stands beside that of the Old King, thus revealing at the same time, as it were, the figures of the preparer and the doer. When Oedipus, blinded and broken, leaves Thebes, his political heir Creon takes his place. Health returns to the city. When Hamlet dies, he takes with him the evil of Claudius and Gertrude. Now Fortinbras becomes a symbol of the new cleanliness. Spring returns to Thebes and Elsinore. For awhile there will be strength. The dramatist makes no promise that the good condition will last forever; this is just one turn in the ceaseless revolution of the seasons. Those of us who can see farther than the limits of these plays as presented know what will happen when the new King Creon suffers a decay. One does not have to look very sharply to see traits in the impetuous Fortinbras which may become serious flaws when he, in his turn, must struggle for the Summer forces it is his function as king to champion. But, says the dramatist, while we have a Spring let us rejoice in it! And maybe, who knows, maybe something from this Spring *will* last.

Generally speaking, the plays which have been most successful have been those in which the protagonist has been made to complete fully all steps of the ritual. He begins at some elevation of Summer. He sinks. He proceeds into Winter and passes all the way through that period so that his flaw may be taken wholly from him. If he is rescued by the playwright this side of the finished purging, the audience may be pleased in a sentimental way about his escape, but it cannot help feeling at the same time a measure of its own defeat. It has been cheated of its cleansing.

Plays with this lack are common today. We see them frequently on the stage. We see them more often in the movies—especially in those originally serious works which are rewritten with a "happy ending" so that they will fit the special tastes of a very young and weak-hearted audience. We see also works of a contrary trend, plays in which the drama *ends* in Winter. They are not as common as the others, but they are equally unsatisfying. They have their purging, but it produces none of the healthful results we have learned to look for in such action. For what purpose is there a cleansing if it does not lead to a new beginning?

Characteristic of the best of tragedy is a close which shows a hope. A strong young shoot has sprouted. The King will rise again, or a stalwart son will take his place. Whatever he is in the story—glorious prince or lowly beggar—he will press forward the struggle for a richer, a more abundant exercise of the life powers. Oedipus has his successor in Creon; Hamlet has his in Fortinbras.

But how about Willie Loman? He too has a son. Willie gives his life that Biff may rise. But how much of a New King does Biff promise to be? His mind is being clarified; his will is being fortified. But he is a kleptomaniac; he is restless; he seems to be incapable of sinking his roots for long in any soil and allowing himself to grow. Is there any real hope that Biff will have a good future to look forward to? The last words of Linda are, "We're free! We're free!" but they are said with a sob, and the spectator knows that the freedom she speaks of is only a freedom for grief.

For hope, then, there must be first a belief that to this troubled life a Summer *can* come and second that human beings *can* possess the wisdom and will to control its coming. Ours is a time of questioning and many of our more sensitive and honest writers, among them Eugene O'Neill and Arthur Miller, do not know clearly just where nor how the light will be seen. Nevertheless they do feel that there is, there must be somewhere, an underlying fire in this dark universe which can create light, and they write about man's search for it. For that we should honor them and all the other dramatists like them. They may not be complete artists, but even with their limitations they are very moving.

If one were to analyze like an Aristotle the prevailing drama of today one would conclude that it contains three principal elements. First is the dynamic search with which we have been dealing in this book. The second is human portraiture with which modern writers are very much concerned; and the third is a cry of pain which, in its strongest form, becomes a threnody, a song of dying.

Playwrights are by the nature of their interests concerned with similitude. Many of our present authors are *especially* interested in this. In an age when they are not very sure about their own inner purposes and therefore cannot do a great deal about putting purpose into their protagonists, they tend to point their attention to aspects of human reporting. So we have today many such works as *Life With Father*, *Life With Mother*, *Our Town*, *Liliom*, *The Man Who Came to Dinner*, and in a more serious mood, *What Price Glory*, *Street Scene*, *The Last Mile*, *Dead End*, and the others like them. Ours is outstandingly a period of recording. We have it not only on the stage but also in the films, radio, and television. Some of it is excellent. Such masters of the theatre as Maxim Gorki, Gerhart Hauptmann, and their imitators in this country are essentially reporters, skillful, understanding, and sympathetic. But they are outside of the main tradition of drama because their plays contain little of the factors of ritual and myth. The characters in their plays begin small and they remain small throughout the limited action in which they are permitted to participate.

Sometimes the reportorial type of portraiture is presented just for itself alone. Often, however, it is employed as a means for the sounding forth of pain. Certain modern playwrights are interested in man, not so much in the form in which he has existed through the ages as in the character he has assumed since the coming of the three questioners of the free spirit, Darwin, Marx, and Freud. Man trapped by his inheritance and environment, man snared by his glandular secretions, man bound by his sex cravings, man crushed by machines and by the society he has created around these monsters—this they view. So our theatre is filled with the wail of yearning but lost people. The "realists," straight portrait painters, and the "expressionists," super-portrait painters, tend to be singers of death songs. Chekhov, in *The Sea Gull* and *The Cherry Orchard*, is a threnodist. August Strindberg, in both *Countess Julie* and *The Dream Play*, is a threnodist. Eugene O'Neill in such works as *Dynamo*, *Strange Interlude*, and, especially, *The Iceman Cometh*, is another threnodist. In *The Hairy Ape*, Yank, speaking to the beast in the cage, cries out:

> I ain't got no past to tink in, nor nothin' dat's comin', on'y what's now—and dat don't belong . . . I ain't on oith and I ain't in heaven, get me? I'm in the middle tryin' to separate 'em, takin' all de woist punches from bot' of 'em. Maybe dat's what dey call hell, huh? . . . . What de hell! T'hell wit it! A little action, dat's our meat! Dat belongs! Knock 'em down and keep bustin' 'em till dey croaks yuh wit a gat—wit steel![3]

Still another outstanding threnodist, but of a different kind, is Tennessee Williams. Most of his people are cultured—at the other end of the ladder up which Yank looks so enviously. The songs they sing are genteel, but the subjects are equally as lost as the rough stoker of *The Hairy Ape*. In *Camino Real* the delicate Marguerite speaks the feelings of all those who suffer with her in her little pocket of existence:

> What are we sure of? Not even of our existence. . . !
> And whom can we ask the questions that torment us?
> "What is this place?" "Where are we?"—a fat old
> man who gives sly hints that only bewilder us more,
> a fake of a Gypsy squinting at cards and tea-leaves.
> What else are we offered? The never-broken procession

> of little events that assure us that we and strangers about us are still going on! Where? Why? And the perch that we hold is unstable! We're threatened with eviction, for this is a port of entry and departure, there are no permanent guests! . . . . We're lonely. We're frightened. We hear the streetcleaners' piping not far away.

Then she adds, because she and those around her desperately need affection:

> Now and then, although we've wounded each other time and again—we stretch out hands to each other in the dark that we can't escape from—we huddle together for some dim-communal comfort.[4]

Let no one say that the drama in the reportorial and threnodic plays is inferior work. Through the best of it man is shown as important, as a creature worthy of being cherished and honored and who *should* be free. Some of these plays attain to considerable poetic power. Still the truth remains that the plays with the biggest dramatic impact have always been and will always be those which take the spectator through suffering to a sense of development on the other side. In modern drama there are many works that do this. Among them are Ibsen's *A Doll House* and Shaw's *Saint Joan*. One of them is Maxwell Anderson's *Elizabeth the Queen*. Others are his *Winterset* and *Key Largo*. Still others are Robert Sherwood's *Abe Lincoln in Illinois*, Lillian Hellman's *Watch on the Rhine*, Paul Green's *Johnny Johnson*, Louis Coxe and Robert Chapman's *Billy Budd*, and Marc Connelly's *Green Pastures*, which, although a fantasy, is fundamentally serious drama. In the protagonists of all these plays is a compelling reach which prevents them, even under the pressure of intense suffering, from finally accepting defeat. In the end they learn something, attain to something, which was never theirs before. They transcend their pain. Though each passes into a temporary Winter, he has at the close a resurgence of vitality. Similar upswings though in a different pattern are to be found in the outdoor works of Paul Green and Kermit Hunter: *The Lost Colony*, *The Common Glory*, *Wilderness Road*, *Unto These Hills*, and *Horn in the West*—epics of men's struggle with, and mastery of, the raw forces of the wilderness, social oppression, and especially the turmoil of human souls. There are many more plays like these even in this present doubting age which show that the ancient tradition of dramatic resurrection is still active.[5]

Some of Eugene O'Neill's plays end in darkness. His best have in them a sturdy glimmer of light. Among those which close with hope are *The Great God Brown*, *Lazarus Laughed*, *Strange Interlude*, and *The Fountain*. The last moments of the grim *Long Day's Journey into Night* are suffused with love and that in effect is a kind of light. Perhaps the most powerful of all of O'Neill's compositions is *Desire Under the Elms*. It is a sombre drama, full of loneliness, greed, and physical passion. The characters of old Ephraim Cabot, his young wife, Abbie, and his son, Eben, start small but they grow. They fight with one another, they nearly destroy each other, they go through a hell of torment together; but in the end they reach a purification of themselves. When the sheriff comes to take Abbie after the murder of her baby, Eben decides to go with her. They walk from the house and toward the outside gate, and when Eben quietly takes her hand a new love springs between them, clean and strong and no longer fearful.

The yearning hero of *All God's Chillun Got Wings* goes through a like Winter. For a time it seems as if all that he has sought in his struggle toward self-fulfillment—an honorable profession in law, a secure position in society and, especially, the affection of the woman he has made his wife—will be crushed in frustration. He fails his examinations, he is shunned by his friends, and the mind of Ella reverts to a state of pitiful childishness. Even the hard walls of his little apartment which was to have been their home seem to shrink around him. Yet he too finds something which shows him the way to peace. He learns how to make an adjustment with those facts of life which he knows must be his, from which he cannot escape, but which he can now embrace without terror. The play ends in a kind of ecstasy.

Ella

And you'll never, never, never, never leave me, Jim?

Jim

Never, Honey.

Ella

'Cause you're all I've got in the world—and I love you, Jim.

(*She kisses his hand as a child might, tenderly and gratefully.*)

Jim

(*Suddenly throws himself on his knees and raises his shining eyes, his tranfigured face.*)

Forgive me, God—and make me worthy! Now I see Your Light again! Now I hear Your Voice!

(*He begins to weep in an ecstasy of religious humility.*) Forgive me, God, for blaspheming You! Let this fire of burning suffering purify me of selfishness and make me worthy of the child You send me for the woman You take away!

ELLA

(*Jumping to her feet—excitedly*)

Don't cry, Jim! You mustn't cry! I've got only a little time left and I want to play. Don't be old Uncle Jim now. Be my little boy, Jim. Pretend you're Painty Face and I'm Jim Crow. Come and play!

JIM

(*Still deeply exalted*)

Honey, Honey, I'll play right up to the gates of Heaven with you!

(*She tugs at one of his hands, laughingly trying to pull him up from his knees as the curtain falls.*)[6]

If Arthur Miller fumbled a little in his making of the final images of *Death of a Salesman*, his hand was steady in *The Crucible*. The play has certain weaknesses in its early parts—some of the motivating forces are not sufficiently drawn—but the end is clear and firm. It fulfills completely the classic tradition that something should rise out of sacrifice. Proctor, the hero, stands in front of the deputy governor of Massachusetts with a confession of witchcraft which Proctor knows is false. If Proctor releases the paper which he holds in his hand his life will be spared. Beside him is the old nurse, Rebecca, likewise accused and likewise innocent. Around him are both friends and enemies. Proctor's wife Elizabeth who has been estranged from him stands watching him, and as she listens to his answers her admiration for him grows. He has shown some hesitancy before but now he is strong.

DANFORTH

(*Pointing at the confession in Proctor's hand*)
You will give me your honest confession in my hand, or I cannot keep you from the rope.
(*Proctor does not reply.*)
Which way do you go, Mister?
(*His breast heaving, his eyes staring, Proctor tears the paper and crumples it, and he is weeping in fury, but erect.*)

DANFORTH

Marshal!

HALE

Man, you will hang! You cannot!

PROCTOR

(*His eyes full of tears*)
I can. And there's your first marvel, that I can. You have made your magic now, for now I do think I see some shred of goodness in John Proctor. Not enough to weave a banner with, but white enough to keep it from such dogs.
(*Elizabeth, in a burst of terror, rushes to him and weeps against his hand.*)
Give them no tear! Tears pleasure them! Show honor now, show a stony heart and sink them with it!
(*He has lifted her, and kisses her now with great passion.*)

REBECCA

Let you fear nothing! Another judgment waits us all!

DANFORTH

Hang them high over the town! Who weeps for these, weeps for corruption!

(*He sweeps out past them.*)

. . . .

HERRICK

Come, man.

(*Herrick escorts them out, Hathorne and Cheever behind them. Elizabeth stands staring at the empty doorway.*)

PARRIS

(*In deadly fear, to Elizabeth*)

Go to him, Goody Proctor! There is yet time!

(*From outside a drumroll strikes the air. Parris is startled. Elizabeth jerks about toward the window.*)

PARRIS

Go to him!

(*He rushes out the door, as though to hold back his fate.*)

Proctor! Proctor!

(*Again a short burst of drums*)

HALE

Woman, plead with him!

(*He starts to rush out the door, and then goes back to her.*)

Woman! It is pride, it is vanity.

(*She avoids his eyes, and moves to the window. He drops to his knees.*)

Be his helper!—What profit him to bleed? Shall the dust praise him? Shall the worms declare his truth? Go to him, take his shame away!

ELIZABETH

(*Supporting herself against collapse, grips the bars of the window, and with a cry*)

He has his goodness now. God forbid I take it from him!

(*The final drumroll crashes, then heightens violently. Hale weeps in frantic prayer, and the new sun is pouring in upon her face, and the drums rattle like bones in the morning air.*)[7]

Proctor with his faults of reticence and indecision dies, but a new essence of him, the image of his sturdy honesty, stands up tall in the community. It will endure and it will be effective.

And yet there is a strange tendency today to mistrust any kind of writer—the poet and novelist as well as the playwright—who includes the concept of Summer in his composition! One can have with more justice a comparable feeling about those persons who too persistently attach themselves to Winter. The works pertaining to this season of death often have a darkly sensuous appeal, and this has attracted many people. Not infrequently the sensation exploited is that of sheer pain to be enjoyed for its own perverse sake. Maeterlinck's *Péléas and Mélisande*, for example, is unquestionably a finely written play. The fact is, however, that it tends to be the special darling of people one suspects of being somewhat sterile in their thinking or still too young to feel the full inner urge of creation. Unable to stir themselves in their desires for either enlargement or preservation they turn, in boredom, to what is most ready to cause a quick, emotional thrill. That always is pain. For this reason they take a delight in watching any kind of dissolution, provided it is rapid and intense enough to prick their senses sharply.

The Lower Depths is a classic of grim characterization. *The Duchess of Malfi* is a superb study of moods. *The Daughter of Jorio* is filled with imagery. *The Cenci* has many poetic qualities. When one can enjoy these plays for their particular, limited virtues they are well worth seeing. Spectators who wish to see them over and over, however, in order to bathe themselves in the peculiarly dark sensations they draw from them are subject to question. It is easy, very easy, to mistake a latent urge of cruelty (toward others or toward oneself) for the whole dramatic response. Sadism and masochism have a questionable part in the normal progress of the seasonal ritual.

The same kind of reservations can be expressed regarding the theatre world of such men as Tennessee Williams. *27 Wagons Full of Cotton* seems to be almost a reveling in pain and those who see great beauty in its performance may have in mind a very special kind of beauty. Even the much finer *A Streetcar Named Desire* may be blemished because the heroine comes into the play without hope and without any means for regenerating herself. In the critical moment when she is left alone with her brother-in-law while her sister is absent having a baby, her final degradation is effected without her even having a chance to defend herself. Too much enjoyment of this kind of drama in our present-day playhouses makes them kin to the ancient Colosseum.

As a balance to plays of this kind people need to see such works of lyrical affirmation as Stephen Benét's *The Devil and Daniel Webster* and to chant along with the great orator facing the spirits from hell:

> There is sadness in being a man, but it is a proud thing too.
> There is failure and despair on the journey—the endless journey of mankind.
> We are tricked and trapped—we stumble into the pit—but out of the pit we rise again.
> No demon that was ever foaled can know the inwardness of that—only men, bewildered men.[8]

The plays of darkness which have survived longest are those which have light as well as darkness. They have a glimmer of sunshine saved for the close. They are not "happy-ending" pieces—hothouse products, not-normal growths—but healthy organisms; they suggest somehow the continuity of living. Summer, Winter, Summer again, thus the great forces move. The best of drama, that which has been most hardy through the centuries, is the kind which fulfills the age-old pattern of the warring seasons, expressed through the figures of a dying and re-arising King.

V. *The Drama of Change*

SLOWLY AUTUMN moves into winter. The last of the leaves fall from the trees, the nights grow cold, frost appears on the windows, and the snow comes softly. People go about their work and their recreations without much reference to the weather. Then suddenly, there is a day when all is different. The sun shines warmly. The air is still. The jonquil buds, which have till now been almost unnoticed, burst wide open. "Spring!" People shout it to each other across the street. The puppies and cats and boys and girls run along the sidewalks and tumble in the yards. There has come a change!

Gradual alterations never receive much attention; everyone becomes accustomed to them. It is the quick shifts which compel notice.[1] A meek little man with pale eyes and stooped shoulders has clerked for many years in a store run by a nagging employer. He has taken the abuse of the other man docilely; not once has any of his acquaintances heard him raise his voice. After each burning tirade he has smiled humbly, gone back to work behind his counter, and said nothing. Then one day, with the store full of people, the little clerk stands his ground; he shouts back at the man who has tormented him.

Something must be done now, quickly! But how will it be done? That question causes a holding of breath; the suspense makes excitement.

The trial of a man accused of committing an unusually brutal crime has drawn to a close. The court is full of onlookers: friends of the murdered man, newspaper reporters, interested citizens. The judge delivers to the bowed prisoner a long and severe sentence which, to everyone present, sounds eminently fair in view of the shocking evidence disclosed. The court is beginning to clear—when the prosecuting attorney rises tremblingly, asks for attention, and states that he is the criminal.

Now what will the lawyer do? What will the judge do? The force of these questions is felt by the focal figure, by the challenger, and by the onlookers. Often it is the onlookers who are the most stirred of all.

This event might occur, of course, not in real life but in a play. Here the principal onlookers are the audience, and the dramatic effect includes them. As a matter of fact, the audience is the one *real* factor in the situation. Since the protagonist and his questioner have their roles only by imagination, the audience is the one body which actually feels dramatic emotion.

Change, then, is the basis of drama. Dramatic art deals with changing human conditions and with people's changing adjustments to them. It deals particularly with the *feelings* produced in people by these changes—by imagination in the character on the stage and really in the spectator watching him from out front. Usually the feelings produced in the two persons are in spirit similar, for the spectator's imagination tends to move as a shadow with every shift of the character's experience. Occasionally, the feelings are different. What is finally important in every case is the effect made on the spectator, the person for whom the drama is designed.

There is a scene in Paul Green's historical play, *The Lost Colony*, which illustrates quite clearly how a quick change of condition and the readjustment forced by it produce a similar feeling in the stage character and the spectator. A group of English colonists sent by Sir Walter Raleigh to Roanoke Island in the new world are gathered before the open chapel in their fort. They have just received the joyful news of the birth of a little girl, Virginia Dare. In the sunlight of the late summer afternoon they kneel reverently to offer their thanks; the priest on the steps before the altar is intoning a prayer. Suddenly, from the rampart above comes the cry of a sentinel. "Indians!" There is a gasp. The women scream and the men rush for their guns.

The effect of the cry is electric; it produces a shock in both the acting colonists on the stage and the observing spectators in the audience. The evident response of the colonists increases the effect of change in the spectator.

Contrasting with this scene of large, essentially physical readjustment is an intimate psychological one in *The Little Foxes*. Horace Giddens, suffering from a critical heart ailment, is in a wheel chair in the sitting room of his home. His wife, Regina, seated near him has been telling him slowly how she has never loved him. He is visibly shaken. As she continues, he puts his hand to his throat. Regina informs him that she knows he will die, and she will be lucky. He reaches tremblingly for a bottle of medicine and a spoon, but drops the bottle and spills its contents. Hoarsely he asks Regina to call the maid. She does not move. In her cold eyes he sees that the end has come.

Here again the effect is electric. Horace tries desperately to make an adequate adjustment, but he and the spectator know that the effort is futile. For Regina, in the play, the sense of change is more limited. Conceivably she has for some time prepared herself for her husband's death and now finds this final moment in the long sequence not so very different from those which preceded it. For her there is an effect, but only a partial one. That, however, is not true of the audience. It sees suddenly for the first time the complete color of Regina's mind, and that revelation causes a sharp readjustment in the spectator's attitude toward her.

A pointed change in a spectator's feeling caused by a pointed change of condition on the stage constitutes then the "dramatic effect." Such an effect commonly springs from a major change, but it can be made by something quite small. What finally causes the heightened state of excitement is always a *shift* of stimulation. And it must be quick.[2] A person adjusted to the sense of warmth, or light, or just the color white is physically unprepared for, and therefore strongly affected by, a sudden sense of cold, or darkness, or the sight of black; that is, the appearance of the one after the other is dramatic.

What occurs strikingly in the physical world occurs similarly, of course, in the mental. A smart recognition, the snap of a new idea, or the rush of a joyous thought is as impressive in its place as the sound of an explosion or the shock caused by the prick of a needle. They, like the simple sensory stimulations, cause one to catch one's breath, flex one's hand, or tighten the muscles of one's calves and thighs. When a political orator seems to be arguing at length against a piece of proposed legislation, then reveals suddenly that he will vote for it; when an apparently normal person talks glowingly about the world of sight, then informs the listener that he is blind; when a friend seems to be dressing one down in particularly violent tones, then winks good humoredly—the effect is exciting. It has in it the essence of drama.

The quick twist at the end of a humorous proverb is a good illustration in miniature of one type of mental reversal:

> It is a sure sign that someone has been thinking about you—when you find a tack in your chair.

There is a nonsense rhyme which has the same kind of turn:

> I stood on the bridge at midnight
> In the cold and frosty air.
> Someone pushed the bridge away
> And left me standing there.

A good example of dramatic mental effect is what happens in the scene between the Nurse and Juliet in *Romeo and Juliet* when the young girl is trying to get her lover's message. The older woman has been complaining at length about her headache and her back pains and Juliet is almost frantic.

JULIET

Sweet, sweet nurse, tell me what says my love?

NURSE

Your love says, like an honest gentleman, and a courteous, and a handsome, and I warrant, a virtuous—Where is your Mother?

Generally what causes a dramatic effect is a shift from a state of lower vitality (sometimes conceived as tension) to a higher one, or the reverse. That is why the sight of the color white after black, or black after white, is arresting. That is why a sudden noise or a sudden silence gets attention. That is why also a quick rise or a quick fall in the "fortunes" of the hero of a play makes good theatre. Hamlet has just turned wearily from his conversation with his uncle when his friends rush in to tell him about the Ghost. Nora Helmer is playing happily with her children when the trouble-maker, Krogstad, enters. The Emperor Jones is boasting to the trader about his enviable security, when he hears the first sound of the drum beating his doom.

In all of the incidents described in this chapter the participant experiences an alteration in his sense of effective living. The clerk in the store was bound by the will of his employer. Now he has burst his bonds and, for a moment at least, he is free. But the story is not ended. Will he be bound again? Will the urge toward a more extensive use of his powers—driven by the restless protoplasm of which he is composed—be finally fulfilled? Or will it be frustrated, perhaps even more tightly now than it was before? Involved in the situation is a doubt as to which will win: something of living, something of Summer? or something of dying, something of Winter? What will be the outcome of the present conflict is important to the onlooker as well as to the clerk because the onlooker cannot help projecting a question regarding the fate of his own vitality into the condition of the other person. In the triumph of the little man he is watching, the spectator will feel some comfort for his own future, in his failure some fear for his own security.

The lawyer in the courtroom was free physically but hemmed in mentally. Now that he has confessed he has, in effect, reversed this condition. But he has weighed the alternatives and decided that his present action will give him in the end a greater sense of freedom. Is he right? Will the muscles, the nerves, and the brainy matter which give substance to the lawyer's spirit rejoice when they sense the response of those who have listened to his words?

The sudden cry of danger in *The Lost Colony*, the cruel statement by Regina in *The Little Foxes*, the teasing of the nurse in *Romeo and Juliet*, and the various turns of fortune in *Hamlet*, *A Doll's House*, and *The Emperor Jones* likewise are connected with threats to vitality. The kinds of vitality that are challenged differ, of course, from scene to scene, but the fundamental factors there are all the same: something of living, something of dying. What makes watching the events so exciting is always the question as to whether the principals in them can make a *good adjustment*, and whether they can make it *in time!*

Any person to become effectively the protagonist of a dramatic composition must be first of all a man or woman *capable of change*. He cannot be so unemotional as not to care about change, too stupid to see the need for change, nor too stolid to act out a change if one seems advisable.[3] When the dramatist has selected an individual who is flexible, ready for change, he puts him into a condition ripe for it: (a) a little too high, or too low, in fortune for it to seem right—according to the spectator's code of poetic justice—for the character to maintain that position indefinitely without challenge; and (b) a little too peaceful, or too happily active, for his condition to seem quite natural in this unstable world. Now the dramatist can disturb his balance by a thrust from some force in his environment, and the man will strive to regain his poise.[4]

All in all, the most dramatic changes are not those which involve just alterations in physical condition or in mental condition, but those which combine both and with them the soul of a man, in other words his complete human organism.[5] A forcible arrest, a murder, a suicide, stunning news brought by a messenger, a woman's unexpected smile which can turn the whole course of a man's life—they are the kinds of changes which make the deepest impression in the end. And the more they involve the man not as just a detached individual but as a part of society the more potent is the effect they produce. The arrest, the murder, the suicide, even the smile, make reverberations which alter a little the whole balance of the earth.

The great reversals in drama—the expansions and contractions, the surgings and recedings—are related to the concept of rotating existence, the rise and fall of the seasons, of daylight, and of the biological life forces. Sunshine and darkness, summer and winter—these are connected in men's minds with the flow and ebb of their own powers; they are part of the same cosmic design. Human creatures caught in the cycle of living and dying are sensitive to the great changes, and to the efforts of other beings' striving so to progress in the circle that their bodies, and especially their souls, do not stop in death. The driving urges of protoplasm to survive and to grow make both the substance of drama and the plot for drama.

While all of the most effective dramatic compositions have in them something of the natures of the four seasons, each tends to stress one certain segment of the cycle. It has in it a "tide." There are works which emphasize the exercise and the enjoyment of human powers; these are the Summertide plays. There are others which point at the loss of powers; they belong to Winter. Spring and Fall dramas are those which deal most strongly with a rising into Summer or a sinking from it. In the Springtide play the sap of life is rising; bodies grow, spirits leap. Labor is good and dangers are welcomed, because this is the time of adventure. The young soldier struggles for his kingdom. Cinderella seeks her Prince.

The action of the Falltide drama starts characteristically in a period of the protagonist's career when for a moment life seems to have reversed a downward trend and to be moving upward. It is a time of false surge, sometimes called an "autumn-spring." The hero is depicted as climbing. (His actions show an upward movement, but one later discovers that a spot of weakness has already found a place in him. He cannot long maintain his climb.) Macbeth, when his story begins, is rising toward kingship; he reaches a peak of his ambition before his greed and fear drag him downward. Othello is elevated to the command of the Venetian forces; Agamemnon is given a triumphant homecoming. Yank declares himself to be lord of the world of steam power. Then comes the disillusionment and the fall toward Winter. The change is dramatic.

Sometimes the plays of Falltide start more gently in a period of "Indian Summer," like Hedda Gabler's. There is no sharp rise at the beginning, but the air is warm and the earth looks peaceful. Into this tranquility a cold wind blows sharply and the true Fall begins. The protagonist then seeks to change the course of the seasons and fight his way back to Summer, or he plunges headlong into Winter hoping to pass through it to a Spring beyond.

The plays which belong most clearly to the Wintertide of the year are those which deal predominantly with darkness. A ready example is Gorki's *The Lower Depths.* Another is O'Neill's *The Iceman Cometh.* In this category belong also the dramas of such Naturalists as the early Hauptmann, such Expressionists as Georg Kaiser, and such designers of nightmare scenes as Strindberg and Wedekind. The protagonists in these pieces are defeated from the beginning; they have no hope except in illusory dreams. But Winter is rightfully not just the time of death. While it is the grave of the year it is also the womb. During the period of cold and snow and the long black nights the brown seeds lying in the earth are forming, nourishing, the little green buds which will press upward in the Spring. So there are dramas of Winter which deal with the gestation of the human spirit, its slow, steadfast resistance to forces of death and its preparation for regeneration when the time of darkness has passed.

If one looks over the long procession of the ages one observes that the most dynamic, and therefore the most effectively dramatic, works tend to be those which are associated, predominantly, not with the height or the depth of the seasonal cycle, but with Spring and Autumn—those parts which are in transition. In the Mid-Summer of Man's spirit his desires reach a certain satiety, and he therefore has little compelling urge to move on. In Winter his soul is often affected by a numbness which allows him little will to change. In the rising tide toward

Summer, however, he is filled with hope and the prospect of struggle is sweet. In the period of sinking, man fights to retain what he has, and he strives mightily to keep away the shadow of the darkness which threatens to close on his desires.

It is interesting to speculate why the dramas which emphasize Fall seem to have a greater permanent attraction than those which revolve around Springtime. One reason may be that fear is ever more immediate in its effect than hope. Another may exist in the fact that, as has already been suggested, a fundamental desire to rid oneself of the feeling of human inadequacy is so pressing that one's mind tends to search for and linger on the dramas with hero-scapegoats. There is no purging in the Spring. The Spring play tends to be short in its elements of ritual.

Perhaps another reason lies in the restless inclination of man to dream, not of the near and not-very-convincing future, but of the distant time. "Tomorrow will be better," he says. But the coming Spring will be better still! Hope can soar higher, can press harder on the senses, than realization. Reality has limits, hope has none.

VI. *Myth and the Hero*

THE TWO PRIMAL ELEMENTS of traditional theatre, as has been stated, are the Ritual of the Seasons and Myth. The nature of the Ritual is clearly biological; Myth is commonly a little less earth-rooted.

A summary of that part which the element of Ritual has played in the growth of drama must emphasize three factors. First is the combat between the forces of Summer and Winter: Summer representing "light," what is related to vitality and order, the release and the organization of powers which make for more effective living; and Winter, "darkness," whatever tends toward frustration and disintegration. There may be occasions, of course, when two "lights" are set against each other, such as the two loyalties, one to the state and one to the family, which trouble the heroine in the ancient drama *Antigone*. But in the course of action one of these must assume the position of a higher "light," casting the other by contrast into shadow and making it for the period of the play a kind of "darkness." Antigone picks the loyalty to family and fights out her battle on that line. There are two "lights" in the modern drama *Winterset*: Miriamne's love and Mio's wish to vindicate his father's honor. Love becomes ascendent because Mio finds that his effort to vindicate has turned into revenge and it no longer contains the spirit of the honor his father stood for. So the age-old pattern of the Winter-Summer struggle is maintained.

The second traditional factor of the Ritual is the arrangement of principals into a relationship of King-and-Scapegoat and King's Son with an opposing spirit of darkness. The first figure, possessing certain admirable qualities of energy and desire, becomes in effect a symbol of man's search for a place in the universe. He is a King because his qualities are drawn larger than those of the people around him—he is an extension, an idealization, of them. He is not a base but a royal representative of mankind. His rise and fall becomes for the observer the rise and fall of everyone. In the course of drama the King shows a weakness—some failure of command over his existence—which hinders his struggle. The King's debility seems to the spectator to be his debility too. Into a physical or spiritual "death" the figure on the stage takes vicariously from those around him a sense of fault similar to his own, purging them of their fault with his. Thus he makes the way clean for a rebirth of royal strength (a "resurrection") in his own person (or in that of a Prince who follows him) and so in the community affected by his presence.

The third factor of the Ritual is the sense of change. The vital seeking for a better condition goes forward or it slips backward. It moves toward Summer or falls toward Winter. This shifting is absorbing to the spectators because in the alterations of condition in the people in the play the spectators feel a turning of their own evolutionary progress toward better adjustment. The changes become truly dramatic when the twists are swift and compressed, when they have about them a sense of urgency.

Myth, the second fundamental element of drama, though its form is now sometimes divergent from the form of the Ritual, is still related to it. Myth grew out of the Ritual. Some of its roots are still there. It has a separate entity mostly in the fact that it is often regarded in the absence of the Ritual, and it has drawn around itself certain traditions which are peculiarly its own. What is associated with Myth has godlike qualities. An animal creature can have no part in Myth. Man can.

Myth may affect many or all of the characters in a play —it frequently does—but its chief concentration is in the two persons of the protagonist and the antagonist. Practically, the protagonist is the same man as he who serves as Ritual's King of the Life Force. Originally conceived, like the King, as a symbol of fertility the Myth element has come gradually to stand for something more illusive. The hero as Myth has spiritual as well as physical qualities. He is a dreamer and thinker as well as doer.

Says Edmund Sinnott of those inner urges which make man aspire: "These passionate and imaginative longings for something higher than he yet has found are the expression of man's spirit. This is a great and mysterious thing. It is no minor or accessory part of him but essential for his very life. Its values are the highest that he knows. The universe comes to flower not in atoms or galaxies but in poets and philosophers, in scientists and saints."[1] Here is something of the essence of Myth as it emerges from Ritual. The Myth figure is a reaching figure. It seeks to extend itself beyond the earth from which it sprang.

The protagonist of drama is touched with Myth—and thereby attains to the power of high drama—when he is associated with, or when he recalls to mind, human figures who have possessed in abundance the qualities here described. The remembered figure now used as inward reference may be a Moses exalted for his leadership or a Buddha for his wisdom. He may be a warrior like Robert E. Lee, distinguished for his courage; a statesman like Abraham Lincoln, marked by his patience; an orator like Winston Churchill, eminent in forceful persuasiveness; or a missionary like Albert Schweitzer, loved for his selfless dedication. He may be an artist, a preacher, a doctor, a teacher, an engineer, or a captain of industry. Usually the Myth figure is what we call a "good" man; occasionally he is a scoundrel. If (according to conventional standards) he is "evil," he possesses in compensation certain outstanding virtues of fearlessness, or energy, or intellectual brilliance which make him seem with regard to them "good" indeed. Always the Myth man has stature. He has godlike qualities in the direction he has chosen to move. Thus, about him grow images of strength, images of power to organize, command and push forward, so he becomes a symbol of human effectiveness. The Heroes in the theatre take a place in the company of Myths when the spectator compares them with the shining figures he already looks up to.

This does not mean, of course, that the typical Myth-Hero of today is a duke or a general. Usually he is not. The modern protagonist is no longer measured for size in *all* his parts. He is presented by his creator with a pointing to certain dominant features. Some important side of him is heroic, or wise, or aggressive, or bright, or deeply feeling, and this side has about it an aspect of the great men gone by. Thus the lowly stoker in *The Hairy*

Ape and the poor fisherwoman in *Riders to the Sea* seem to be for a little while very superior people.

If the personalization of the quality of "light" is a Myth figure, so also may be the personalization of "darkness." There can be no size in Faust unless he is compared with a Mephistopheles. In great drama both the protagonist and the antagonist are affected by Myth. Drama is built on struggle. Common drama becomes powerful drama only when conflict has dimension—when the warring enemies in it are both giants.

What in brief are the marks of the Hero—and, in a comparable though perhaps reversed way, of the Villain? First, he is a person of great capacities: he can feel deeply, he can suffer intensely, he can struggle vigorously. He has enough mind to think about his longings, to take joy in his successes, and to be troubled by his failures. In a play involving moral values he must know "sin" and want to be delivered from it. Since he is a feeling man, the Myth-Hero senses profoundly the pulls and drags of the forces around him. He is a discontented individual. He is not satisfied with the state of being in which he exists and has a compulsive desire to improve it. The Myth-Hero is an active rebel.

This person is always moving, for the nature of Myth is never still; men become Myths when they *do* something. Maurice Maeterlinck once tried to make theatre out of an old man resting in a chair, but he abandoned this ill-advised effort when he found that the result was only a picture. The image refused to come alive. Much is said today about the "static drama" of Chekhov. The characters of such works as *The Cherry Orchard* and *The Three Sisters* do not stir far in any one straight line, that is true, but they are not still. They move intensively in small circles, but in doing this they stir up a lot of emotion.[2] Clearly, there can be no drama without change. Change always means action. The hero of a play is ever a man trying to adjust matters, and he cannot be seen as really wanting to do this until he obviously is going into motion in an effort to bring about something different.

Among the elements which give the Hero his peculiar character, the most distinctive is that which men call his "dream." This is the image of what the Hero desires most passionately to have; it is something toward which (during the passage of the drama) he orients his whole body and mind in striving. The force of the dream affects directly the quality of Myth in him. The more compelling the dream, the more vibrant and moving the nature of the Hero—the more there is of Myth about him.

Ever the substance of the dream is a fulfilling action. If in the end the Hero can attain to the experience of that action, he knows he will feel a surge of power, a sense of being organized and united with the heart-stream of universal life. The form of the dream can be many things; it has meaning only as it is related to the Hero's own particular existence. The dream may be centered in the exhilaration of leading a nation in such a way as to reap honor, win wealth, or attain the satisfaction of rendering new and shining services to the citizens. It may be the building of a fine, big ship or a city. It can be the consummation of a wonderful courtship. Says Romeo to Juliet:

> Wert thou as far
> As that vast shore washed by the furthest sea,
> I would adventure for such merchandise.

The dream may be the conquering of a wilderness. It may be the simple but rich enjoyment of a home filled with a thousand little objects which caress the senses and make the person who lives among them feel that, for him, the place is empire.

It is a humble dream like this which motivates the toil of two lonely ranch hands in Steinbeck's *Of Mice and Men*. George speaks often to the childlike Lennie about the farm they long to own: "Got a little windmill. Got a little shack on it and a chicken run. Got a kitchen orchard. Cherries, apples, peaches, 'cots and nuts. Got a few berries. There's a place for alfalfa and plenty water to flood it. There's a pig pen. . . . And we'd keep a few pigeons to go flying round and round the windmill, like they done when I was a kid. And it'd be our own. And nobody could can us. If we don't like a guy we can say: 'Get to hell out,' and by God he's got to do it. And if a friend come along, why, we'd have an extra bunk. Know what we'd say? We'd say, 'Why don't you spen' the night?' And by God he would."[3]

At the end of the play Lennie dies, an outcast of the community and mourned by none except one undistinguished friend. Yet, at the moment of his going, he has a glimpse of glory and that vision makes him kin to the great men of the world.

Striving to achieve an adjustment between man's frailty and the roaring forces of the universe around him, the Myth-touched Hero is usually driven by a hunger for union with an order superior to his own. It may be an order which he perceives in the unified, creative strength of a family, a state, or a brotherhood of man; or it may be in something of the world of nature; or in something still more spiritual beyond the touch of sight and sound. The godlikeness of the Hero's nature here consists, not so much in the state of his present accomplishment, as in the grandeur of his search. The very act of seeking makes within itself an image of the godhead striven for. So the passion to "belong" is one of the most compelling themes in the theatre. It appears in the works of many dramatists old and new, in recent times most notably in the plays of Eugene O'Neill. His protagonists are hunters for a force greater than their own which they feel could give dignity to their existence. Yank in *The Hairy Ape* attempts to find the vital, integrating influence in human friendships. Cabot in *Desire Under the Elms* tries to feel it in the warm strength of his farm. Brown in *The Great God Brown* seeks it in the genius of creation. The Reverend Hutchins Light in *Dynamo* expects, but fails, to grasp it in the power of a great machine; while John Loving in *Days Without End* turns for it to the cross. What each of these men looks for is, at heart, God. God is the supreme love, the supreme reason, the supreme organization of those great values for which men yearn.[4]

All of O'Neill's searchers are religious men in the sense in which Herbert J. Muller defines religion. "The root experience," he says, "the experience that makes religious belief precious to sensitive men, appears to be a sense of oneness with an immense whole: a feeling of complete harmony that at crises may lead to a lasting conversion, a coming to final terms with life, and at its most intense is the mystical experience, but that always works to steady and strengthen men's purposes, deepen their sense of values, support their ideal aspirations, enrich the whole significance of their lives."[5] "A man's religion," suggests Gordon W. Allport, "is the audacious bid he makes to bind himself to creation and to the Creator. It is his ultimate attempt to enlarge and to complete his own personality by finding the supreme context in which he rightly belongs."[6]

So the heroes of O'Neill, and of the playwrights like him, are large personalities in the extent of their desire and their courage to assume a relationship with God and of their unceasing endeavor to perfect it.[7]

VII. *Theatre as Adventure*

EVERY HUMAN INDIVIDUAL wants to think and to act *fully*. He wants to be filled with pleasurable emotions and to express these emotions in action which is everywhere effective. Few men in their existence find nearly as much of this experience as they crave; what men do achieve they hold as precious. For it they seek an enduring continuity. They seek stability.

A feeling of stability is, in effect, a feeling of good equilibrium between the personality and his environment—between the personality and his universe—which cannot easily be shaken. Within the compass of this feeling a man's powers can work safely; he knows that his powers are adequate to his situation; he is therefore in a state of peace. That is very much to be desired. But only up to a point. If the powers of the man, however great they may be, are faced with no challenges whatever—can move about too easily—they are very likely to cease exerting themselves at all. If they stop, the man is unhappy again. The active, good emotions cease. When the man's powers are dulled, his spirit is dulled and he is discontented; he can never feel completely alive except when his senses are tingling, his muscles are tensing, and his mind is stirring.

So, besides stability man wants adventure. Adventure arouses the whole person; it provides him with struggle, it calls into play all his faculties. When he is engaged in an enterprise involving a risk he senses more sharply, because he is now on the alert and must distinguish between one stimulus and another. He thinks more keenly, because he must evaluate, plan, and make choices. He must pick quickly between what will lead to a condition of Summer and what will take him to Winter. He moves more lightly ("on his toes") because he must be ready at any moment to do something new, different, daring, hitherto untried.

By nature, by necessity, every normal individual is at least in part an experimenter. He is aware that he must keep his powers so in trim that he can protect and project himself. Adventure provides the active tests. That is why he likes to hunt wild cats, to ride swift horses, and to climb high precipices. That is why he likes to stalk dangerous men and to play games of skill with sharp-brained men. That also is why he is eager to enter a new industrial venture or start a magazine or build an airplane. He wants to try boldly novel sensations, fresh avenues of reasoning, strange emotions. He will investigate the facts of the physical world. He will explore the dark places of the human mind. He will hurl his questions at men in high places. He will pit his strength against other strengths. If man is not finally destroyed by these adventures he emerges from them with a greater understanding and skill, and therefore a greater confidence in his control over himself and his surroundings. He has a richer feeling about his stability for it is a stability founded now, not on accident but on a sense of adequacy.

One of the most effective ways to have an adventure in this imperfect world is to participate in a work of art. Here, in a condition of restless imbalance, are shown various physical and intellectual elements on their way toward a new balance, a new condition of Summer. Here is created a purpose looking toward an adjustment with a challenge to it, a thrust and a counter-thrust, a suspense and a resolution, all designed for the greatest possible amount of activity within a limited space and time.

Art as adventure gives release to human energy. It does something about fulfilling the three great fundamental human urges described in Chapter I. It helps man by imagination to exercise, to preserve, and to enlarge his human powers. Ordinary man in his ordinary life suppresses nine-tenths of his impulses. He does this because he is afraid of them. Since he cannot manage the impulses without confusion he does not give them rein; he curbs his feelings, he curbs his thinking, and he curbs his doing, to be safe. So, instead of being a creature of purposeful action, he drifts. For most of the people most of the time life is a heavy lethargy, not because they choose it to be that, but because they cannot do much to alter it. The artist can. He has traits which make him by nature a more sensitive perceiver of the stimulating factors in the environment and, at the same time, talents, developed by careful training, which make him an especially efficient organizer of responses to those stimuli. Using his gifts of clear perception and orderly response, he is able to lead other men into the release of their pent-up urges and into the pointing of them toward a new pattern of free and balanced action. Thus the artist causes both an exercise and a control of exercise.

In effect, art both celebrates and satisfies man's great sleepless protoplasmic longings. It devotes itself in the end to the problem of solving the paradox of security and adventure, for the two, though related, are opposites. Complete security leads to a feeling of tranquillity, but tranquillity too much indulged in leads to sterility, then to death. The great teacher of the New Testament long ago stated the truth: "Whosoever would save his life shall lose it." The seeds of life lie in change. In the last analysis, then, art is primarily an expression of man's urge to grow. It reflects his rebellion against mere existence and his search for new ways to meet the call of living. Since it stands for change it holds the youthful spirit of man. Settled old age finds little sympathy and little joy in art. Art appeals to the young in heart.

Among the many forms that man has created the one which most pointedly stirs adventurous participation is the theatre. Dramatic art exerts a peculiarly strong influence on an observer because it addresses itself to him in a very direct way. Theatre exploits the visible and audible bodies of moving actors. The settings for a play are imitative, or at least suggestive, of places readily to be seen in the world of reality. The words of the performers and the shapes of their gestures are made out of the same molds as those of the spectator. The story is human. The whole composition is ordered for an immediate effect. If the work of planning is well done, there is action in every moment of it, and the pulse of it beats straight into the tissues of the men and women who are watching it. Theatre is the temple of adventurous living. It is the place where men may experience in the most exhilarating way possible the loss of old equilibriums and the finding of new, better ones. It helps men to use, secure, and expand their powers in a state of vigorous emotion.

John Sebastian Bach once said of music: "It is for the glory of God and a pleasant recreation." This could serve very well as a motto for the theatrical artist, and he would not have to be a religious man in any narrow sense to support it.

The two parts of Bach's dictum are intimately related; if one starts with the premise that the primary purpose of a work of art is "recreation," one must take that word with its original meaning. There can be no "re-creation" without a fundamental creation. Purely sensuous exercise becomes quickly enervating unless it is connected somehow with the great process of evolution, and the inner fact in that is creation. The figure of John Sebastian Bach's "God" stands as a symbol of it.

If God is creator, the Devil is sterility, impotence, the great envious darkness of Winter. The Devil stands for the forces which seek to impede evolution by blocking, tearing at, the live organism. They have their expression in fear, jealousy, hatred, inertia, impulses of destruction and ridicule. The dramatist deals in his composition with both Beings, using them as the inner antagonists of his grand conflict. In order to make contrast and to effect change in his play he sets up a strong Devil, but the heart of his design is a God of Will prepared to fight for a Good. The Good is creative, fulfilled living, the enlargement into the universe of man's physical, mental, and emotional powers. Evil works against that.

The forces of sterility are moving actively in the world today. Doctrines of despair are persuading masses of people to quit struggling for "impractical goals," to give up responsibility as individuals and to become thoughtless, undifferentiated, uncreative units of large will-less masses. Unfortunately, much of the literature of our time—novels, short stories, and poetry—has been affected by this blighted thinking. The one art form which seems still to be most resistant to it is the theatre. This may be because among all the arts, the dramatic is the one which presents the living bodies and voices of actors directly before the senses of the observer, and in the playhouse men wish to see mirrored thus intimately not the sterile but the creative sides of themselves.[1] Usually plays of ultimate despair have been not just critical, but also commercial, failures.

This does not mean that the theatre accepts only romantic brightness. Quite the contrary. The most vigorous period dramatic art has ever known was that which existed in Elizabethan England just before and during the time of Shakespeare. What gave it its wonderfully lasting vitality was its boundless faith in man's potentialities, his ability to act, to think, and to feel heroically. Yet, paradoxically, what we now cherish from that period is not so much the comedies as the tragedies. Though the protagonists in these plays meet death, they live during the time of their adventurous action so intensively that the pain at the end seems small. And always at the close of the adventure is a moment of illumination that makes the incident of death have a kind of glory.

All dramatic writers are, consciously or unconsciously, affected by the great cycle of living and dying. Few of them concentrate on the whole of it at one time and each, according to his temperament, tends to be interested principally in one or another segment of it. One author likes to deal with Springtide, the regeneration; another with Mid-Summertide, the transition from rise to fall; another with Autumntide, the sinking; while still another concerns himself with Wintertide, the period of death, the waiting for the new Spring. Many authors deal with different segments at different points of their career, now exploring a phase of rising, now one of falling. Always, however, the cycle is something in motion. A still cycle is a lifeless one; no dramatist yet has managed to write successfully of humanity standing still.

If one conceives of the cycle of living and dying as a ring of forces, one sees it revolving through the stations of the four seasons—up, over, down the other side, and back again to the starting point. The motion is unceasing, inexorable. The cycle of energies, some pushing, some pulling, cannot be imagined as a neat thin current; the current has a thickness. The great tide moves steadily from spring to summer, to fall, to winter, to spring again. Through the middle of that wide current, however, runs a seething heart stream whose action is affected by present influences—physical events, sources of love and hatred, passing fads of thought. The stream flows sometimes quickly, sometimes slowly, sometimes backward, but mostly forward around the ring. Writers like to observe the whole tide, but especially the heart stream. Those who view the stream close by are the reporters, the realists. Seeing as they do intimately the sweaty turbulent details of life which exist there, they tend to miss the larger form of movement; so they concern themselves with sensual elements and often develop into pessimists.

Some distance away from the stream are the poets and philosophers, the artists of the larger vision. These men are less interested in details for their own sake than they are in the meaningful shapes of them; they watch the forms of the great surging drives up and down along the curve. All the authors, both those near the heart stream and those a little removed, are warmed by the central heat. They compose their plays feelingly under its influence. Some, however, try to get too far away from the stream, out into the atmosphere of reason unclouded by emotion. But out there where they cannot see or listen to the rush of life they seldom write effectively about the stuff of drama. Life and death have ceased to move for them; therefore, they cease to be, in the proper sense of the term, *dramatic* artists.

The ablest playwright includes in his thinking all parts of the life and death cycle. When he makes his protagonist descends into death, the author makes him carry with him the seed of a later awakening. As the writer contemplates his man he sees him at different distances. He observes him nearby, feeling the forces which in daily living tug and push him this way and that. Also he sees the man removed, where he can view the man's relationship to other men and other circumstances. It is true that the author may become especially obsessed with one aspect of the protagonist; but, to make his treatment of him have valid dimension he knows he must suggest the whole man. This includes not only the man's present but also his past and his future; and more than that, his inheritance and that which will some day spring from his ashes. He must be an individual but also a part of whirling humanity.

And the artist *may* feel even more. Many fine playwrights see the circle that is all. A few of the sharpest, observing the ring, note that it does not have a closed orbit but is part of a forward-moving spiral. For them the elements of Spring, Summer, Autumn, and Winter do something besides swinging through the same path year after year. There is always at least a little pushing onward; each spring reaches forward a little beyond the last. The superior artist reckons with man's spirit and inevitably he sees that that spirit is linked with the whole movement of biological life. Edmund Sinnott the scientist says: "By means which still elude us but are the goal equally of the biologist, the poet, and the philosopher are born those yearnings which make man the noble animal he is. Living things are seekers and creators, and striving for goals is the essence of all life; but in man these goals have risen to heights before undreamed of, and he can set them ever higher at his will. Man's feet are planted in the dust, but he lifts his face to the stars." And again: "Not only does life express itself in organized systems of exquisite complexity wherein goals at many levels are attained, but these systems are not static. Their goals are ever changing. Man rides the crest of this advancing wave. His nature and his destiny are ultimately those of life itself, and the longings of his spirit are part of the great upward surge of life from amoeba to man. Who knows how far it still may carry him?"[2]

The cynic has ever cried against this view, calling it unrealistic and sentimental. To support his contentions concerning the essentially evil nature of man, he marshals an imposing array of testimony from the present world and from history. Clearly the spiral of human life is no quickly moving figure and in its stream there are frighteningly powerful eddies moving backwards, backwards toward the darkness from which it tries to escape. But to say that the whole flow is backwards seems to ignore the practical facts of simple biology. The main forces, moving gradually, *are* pressing forward.

One of our leading dramatic poets, Maxwell Anderson, has seen this. In a now-famous passage he states: "From the beginning of our story men have insisted, despite the darkness and silence about them, that they had a destiny to fulfill—that they were part of a gigantic scheme which was understood somewhere, though they themselves might never understand it. There are no proofs of this. There are only indications—in the idealism of children and young men, in the sayings of such teachers as Christ and Buddha, in the vision of the world we glimpse in the hieroglyphics of the masters of the great arts, and in the discoveries of pure science, itself an art, as it pushes away the veils of fact to reveal new powers, new laws, new mysteries, new goals for the eternal dream." Then Anderson defines the dream: "The dream of the race is that it may make itself better and wiser than it is, and every great philosopher or artist who has ever appeared among us has turned his face away from what man is toward whatever seems to him most god like that man may become."[3]

Every adult individual in his normal state is inclined almost fiercely to be a moral person. He could not exist as a social being if he were not. In the eminently gregarious atmosphere of the theatre he wants the characters and the stories in which he participates to reflect his group attitudes toward himself and his fellow men. These feelings have been formed, conditioned, and reconditioned by years of experience as a member of a human herd, and he does not wish now to change them suddenly without good reason. The playwright *can* change the attitudes if he desires, but to do that he must build his deviation on fundamental values even deeper than the surface morality with which the play happens at the moment to be dealing. The mores of a people differ between place and place and from time to time; but there are certain fundamental virtues that are cherished unalterably. They are courage, loyalty, affection between men and women, tenderness toward children, reverence for the honorable, and the will to fight for one's convictions. These are a part of the fibre of human nature the world over, and they have little to do with national laws, theoretical philosophies, or dogmatic religions. The respect for them springs out of man's profound evolutionary urges to develop productively.

The artist regards them lovingly. He is fundamentally forever a lover. The basic virtues are his most valuable assets. When he starts with them he can be sure his foundations are secure. Then it does not matter much whether the composition on which he is working is profound or light, serious or mocking; it will have a right premise. It will be related in the spectator's mind to the conscious stream of human existence, the ceaseless struggling effort of men everywhere to exercise, preserve, and enlarge their powers for the greatest possible enjoyment of living.

Notes

CHAPTER I

1. Washington Matthews (trans.), *Navaho Myths, Prayers, and Songs with Texts and Translations* (University of California Publications in American Archeology and Ethnology, Vol. 5, No. 2, Berkeley: The University Press, 1907), p. 29.

2. Pronounced "Oxi'trika".

3. Protozoan organisms show physiological states which are analogues of the physiological states of pain and fear in man. They show evidence also of a rudimentary memory which helps them adapt themselves in their environment. When Oxytricha has moved from the area of heated water to the cool, it stays there without trying to dart back immediately into the hot. Paramecium, after it has fed itself below the surface of the water, tends to come up and remain there until it is hungry again, when it dives back to the source of its food. It remembers the position of it. Protozoa are teachable. They learn to reject harmful substances and stay near beneficial ones.

4. Herbert J. Muller, *Science and Criticism* (New Haven: Yale University Press, 1943), p. 107.

5. Edmund W. Sinnott, *Cell and Psyche: the Biology of Purpose* (Chapel Hill, N.C.: University of North Carolina Press, 1950), p. 20.

6. *Ibid.*, pp. 23-24.

7. There is no evidence, of course, that the line of evolution to higher creatures actually passes through Oxytricha. In the grand pattern of development there are parts in which little animals do not press forward at all, and others in which they do the opposite, regress. Nevertheless the tendency to go on into more and more complicated states of organization does operate in the primitive animal world. Evolution is a continuing fact. The inherent purposefulness of protoplasm is discussed by Sinnott in *Cell and Psyche*. See Note 12.

8. E. S. Russell, *The Directiveness of Organic Activities* (Cambridge, England: Cambridge University Press, 1945), p. 178.

9. Sinnott, *Cell and Psyche*, p. 76.

10. E. S. Russell, *The Directiveness of Organic Activities*, p. 179.

11. Sinnott, *Cell and Psyche*, p. 72. Some biologists of the purely mechanistic school take issue with the directive theory of Sinnott and his associates. The weight of modern scientific thinking, however, seems to be inclining toward the latter. In recent years the strict materialists have been losing ground.

12. Sinnott, exploring the desires of the human organism in *Cell and*

Psyche, poses the question: "Whence do such strange longings arise? What is there that should make man crave these higher things?" He answers: "To the physiologist this is no mystery. These emotions, passions, and longings of the human spirit, whatever their evolutionary significance may be, must be anchored firmly in the chemistry of protoplasm, in the physiology of the nervous system itself." P. 99.

CHAPTER II

1. Theodor H. Gaster, *Thespis: Ritual, Myth and Drama in the Ancient Near East* (New York: Henry Schuman, 1950), pp. 3-30.

2. Sir James George Frazer, *The Golden Bough* (New York: Macmillan Co., 1952), p. 360.

3. *Ibid.*, p. 380.

4. There is evidence that the legends of the wandering Ulysses, Jason's search for the Golden Fleece, Noah and his ark, Jonah and the whale, Beowulf and the firedrake, and St. George and the dragon are of solar and seasonal origin.

5. The cycle of life and death is reflected benignly in the pattern of a man's waking and sleeping. It is reflected also in those patterns of withdrawal and return that Arnold Toynbee sees in the lives of spiritual leaders such as Jesus, Saint Paul, Saint Benedict, Buddha, and Mohammed; and in the similar behavior of those "creative minorities" which shape the courses of rising and falling civilizations.—Arnold J. Toynbee, *A Study of History* (New York: Oxford University Press, 1947).

6. One of the most interesting of the popular dramatizations evolving from seasonal rituals and myths elsewhere in Europe is the English mummers' play.—Gaster, *Thespis*, pp. 439-43.

7. There seems to be some question now as to whether the liturgical works actually represent the first noteworthy theatrical activity in Europe after the death of Roman drama. Evidence points to mimes and other forms of performance given informally around the country. The church works, however, clearly provide the spur for the literary part of the revival.

8. Jesus said of himself: "I am the resurrection and the life."

9. Sir E. K. Chambers, *The Mediaeval Stage* (Oxford: Oxford University Press, 1903), II, pp. 14, 9. Also George Sampson, *The Concise Cambridge History of English Literature* (New York: The Macmillan Company, 1942), p. 231.

CHAPTER III

1. The terms "Summer" and "Winter" have grown into our language to represent general qualities of good and evil: "He was . . . to those men that sought him, sweet as summer" (Shakespeare). "Shall I compare thee to a summer's day?" (Shakespeare). "The isles of Greece, the isles of Greece! . . . Eternal summer gilds them yet" (Byron). "For him in vain the envious seasons roll who bears eternal summer in his soul" (Oliver Wendell Holmes). "How like a winter hath my absence been from thee" (Shakespeare). "The winter of our discontent" (Shakespeare).

A little rule, a little sway,
A sunbeam in a winter's day
Is all the proud and mighty have
Between the cradle and the grave. (John Dyer)

2. The sun has been established in tradition throughout the world. Hymns and poems to the sun are found everywhere. Typical is the old Egyptian Aton hymn: "When thou settest on the Western horizon, the land is in darkness in the manner of death . . . (but) when the day breaks, as thou risest on the horizon . . . they awake and stand upon their feet . . . they live because thou hast arisen for them." In Greece, Zeus, the god of the Bright-Sky, was worshipped as father. In India, every Brahman repeats daily: "Let us meditate on the desirable light of the divine sun, may he rouse our minds." The east has been regarded in every part of the world as the source of all that men hold dear: light, life, warmth, and happiness. Ancient temples (such as those in Athens and Jerusalem) and Christian churches (the great Cathedral of St. Peter at Rome) have been oriented toward the east. Peoples in numerous countries turn to the east in prayer. Graves and burial rites are related to the east. Children playing such games as " Oats, peas, beans, and barley grow" and "Here we go round the mulberry bush," in various parts of Europe, used to consider it lucky to circle toward the sun or go on the sun-side. In contrast, the ceremonials of the worshippers of Kali, Death Goddess, who belonged to the murderous fraternity of thugs in India, were turned to the west, and covens of witches in Scotland used to dance "widershins," that is in a direction contrary to the apparent course of the sun.

3. The first thing made by God in the Biblical story of creation was light. Jesus brought light to the souls of men: "In him was life; and the life was the light of men." (St. John 1:4.) In the world of animal and human life the search for light begins in the Protozoan, Euglena, at the foot of the evolutionary ladder. At the top, a craving for the precious essence of light is observable in the Christian ceremony of the Feast of Lights.

4. Examples will be found in the plays of Strindberg and Wedekind.

5. R. R. Spencer, "Staying Alive," *Saturday Review of Literature* (Oct. 27, 1951), pp. 40-41.

6. Mammals attack mammals, fish oppose fish, insects eat insects. Even the Protozoa prey on each other. The small but powerful ciliate, *Didinum*, darts here and there, occasionally striking a Paramecium. It buries its proboscis in its victim which it then proceeds to swallow whole. The biologist, Herbert S. Jennings, describes graphically in one of his books a hard-fought battle between two amoebae which he watched through a microscope. The larger amoeba approached the smaller one and swallowed it. Before the smaller amoeba could be assimilated, however, it put forth its pseudopodia and, with an effort, pulled itself free. It tried to swim away, but the larger animal turned, followed it, and again engulfed it. Once more the little amoeba put forth an effort and at the end of a twelve-minute struggle won its freedom.—Herbert S. Jennings, *Contributions to the Study of the Behavior of Lower Animals* (Published by the Carnegie Institution of Washington, 1904), pp. 200-2.

7. R. E. Coker, "Some Philosophical Reflections of a Biologist II," *The Scientific Monthly* (February, 1939), p. 123.

8. Ashley Montagu, *On Being Human* (New York: Henry Schuman, 1950), pp. 31-33.

9. Montagu states that planarian worms which have been exposed to ultraviolet radiation disintegrate more rapidly when isolated than when grouped. Protozoans grow more rapidly when they are introduced into a sterile medium in large numbers than when the cultures are started with only a few organisms. Herring gulls in the bigger colonies commence sexual activities earlier and lay and hatch their eggs faster than those in the smaller ones.—Montagu, *On Being Human*, pp. 39-40.

10. *Ibid.*, p. 99.

11. R. C. Jebb (trans.), *The Complete Greek Drama* (edited by Whitney J. Oates and Eugene O'Neill, Jr., New York: Random House, 1938), I, pp. 381, 404.

12. Quite ironically at the end of the play Mrs. Alving's image of defeat, her son, calls for the sun.

13. Conflict moves the spectator most when it does not develop in a straight line but surges up and down with first one member of the struggle having the advantage, then the other. The most effective forces for making this combat move about are "complications." Complications are side thrusts from other people, objects or forces which alternately help and hinder the protagonist. Striving to reach a position of eminence in public life, perhaps, a man is aided by the encouragement of his wife, temporarily blocked by a fear of his inability, lifted again by some reassuring advice from a friend, driven backwards by the envy of rivals, helped by the unexpected acquisition of some property, tripped by a physical accident, and finally given a boost toward success by a discovery of his own courage. All of these influences are expressed in incidents and they take time; so the conflict is extended over a considerable period. The complications stretch out the fighting. They prevent any kind of quick and easy settlement. In *A Doll's House*, the struggle of Nora is made difficult—and therefore exciting—by many such complications. There are her love for her children and her husband, her pampered upbringing, Torvald's treatment of her as a doll-woman, and her inclination to tell "white lies." These have tended over the years to soften her character and to make fighting hard for her now. Then there are forces not personal to her but working on her: Torvald's blind egotism, Krogstad's need and consequently threatening action, Dr. Rank's untimely expression of his love. Working for Nora is Mrs. Linde's sympathy and her own conviction that she is right. All of these exert influences on the struggle and make the outcome increasingly a matter of question. Similar influences affect the movements of the Prince in *Hamlet.*. Like forces dog the footsteps of Regina in *The Little Foxes.* Driving the courses of the plays this way and that, the complications in each case make the conclusion a matter of exquisite suspense.

CHAPTER IV

1. Gilbert Murray, "Excursus on the Ritual Forms Preserved in Greek Tragedy," in Jane Ellen Harrison's *Themis* (England: Cambridge University Press, 1912), p. 341.

2. The concept of death and resurrection in the classics must be seen broadly. The presence, or the promise, of the new King is usually rather clear in Shakespeare's plays, but the image of this figure is sometimes a little blurred in the Greeks' dramas. At the end of the *Eumenides,* the third work in Aeschylus' *Oresteia,* the form of the reborn prince is obvious. Orestes is freed from the grip of the Furies (a kind of death), he rises in strength, and is blessed. And the Eumenides themselves are delivered from Winter, changed into Summer. The shapes of rebirth in *Agamemnon* and *The Choephori* are less clear. The Chorus in the first play does, however, look forward hopefully to the return of Orestes to right the evil at Argos, and near the close of *The Choephori,* Orestes acquires the strength to avenge his father's death. It is true that he is now beset by the Furies, but he has already effected a major rebirth for Argos, and the leader of the Chorus points his way to the shrine where he will be freed from his new torments. Aeschylus, as a highly religious artist, puts great stress on the moral orderliness of the Universe. Sophocles ends his plays with moderation and some indirection. (In *Oedipus at Colonus* the old king, his life fulfilled, is translated into the next world, a kind of rebirth for him, while his daughters rise up to take his place in this world. In *Antigone,* however, the heroine falls and so do the king and the prince. The figure that rises is an abstract one, Wisdom, invoked by the Chorus.) Euripides tends to lift his endings forcefully, but he has been criticized because he works out his rising action artificially: he makes the universal powers create a resurrection on behalf of man, through the aid of a *deus ex machina,* instead of letting man himself rise within the frame of the universal order.

3. Eugene O'Neill, "The Hairy Ape," *Nine Plays by Eugene O'Neill* (The Modern Library. New York: Random House, Inc., 1932), pp. 86.

4. Tennessee Williams, *Camino Real* (New York: New Directions, 1953), pp. 96-97.

5. It is worth noting that among the seventeen plays picked by the New York Drama Critics Circle as the best works of the period of 1935 to 1956, nine have endings which are frankly forward looking and five more have endings which clearly incline that way. In the seventeen dramas cited for the Pulitzer Prize in the same years the proportion of the forward look is even greater. Only two of the works, *A Streetcar Named Desire* and *The Shrike,* can be described as closing in a condition of lasting darkness.

6. Eugene O'Neill, "All God's Chillun Got Wings," *Nine Plays of Eugene O'Neill* (The Modern Library. New York: Random House, Inc., 1932), pp. 132-33.

7. Arthur Miller, *The Crucible* (New York: Viking Press, 1953), pp. 143-45.

8. Stephen Vincent Benét, *The Devil and Daniel Webster* (New York: Farrar and Rinehart, Inc., 1939), p. 71.

CHAPTER V

1. An unexpected stimulation is alerting, so in a way it is dramatic. Some of the Protozoa are sensitive to sudden changes from light to darkness or darkness to light, but not to gradual changes. Larger animals react in

a similar way. The psychologist, John Frederick Dashiell, calls attention to the effect of change of attention: "The beast of prey stalks its victim, often moving so slowly that it escapes observation until it has gotten within striking distance. An insect crawling on the skin or under the resting hand will excite an attending attitude with an effectiveness out of all proportion to its size. The flitting of a mouse across the periphery of the visual field will turn a dozing cat or dog into an alert and excited hunter. . . . Many a weak and helpless animal, on the other hand, has for one of its most effectual defenses a death feint, a 'playing 'possum,' which renders it so completely motionless that it may escape the notice of its dangerous enemy." —John Frederick Dashiell, *Fundamentals of General Psychology* (Boston: Houghton Mifflin Company, 1937), pp. 330-31.

2. In the theatre, the term, "quick change," has a comparative meaning only. This is especially true of mental change. For the small scale, it may be an immediate shift, such as a pointed turn of subject in a conversation. For the larger scale, however, it will be the movement of a whole train of thought in time. Although such changes may be indicated by a playwright as occupying periods of days, weeks or even months, they are actually perceived by the spectator in a very brief time—from two to two and one-half hours at most. The compression of an experience of this kind which might not seem very striking off the stage gives it a breathtaking quality in the theatre. In effect, the change really is quick.

3. What is called "dramatic action" is in essence dramatic change. Any kind of sharp change, physical or mental, makes action. A single alteration of sensation, or of thought, makes in effect one moment of it. A connected series of such changes makes sustained action. The most powerful agent for continuity is a human drive toward a goal: something must be attained or something must be preserved. As long as the adjustment is still being worked for, the feeling of action is alive. If the thing desired, the goal to be reached, can be realized easily, there are not likely to be along the way any sharp changes of condition which will make for dramatic effect. Consequently, there will be no genuine sense of action. This is altered, however, if the adventure of achievement is attended by difficulties. The more intense the difficulties and the more continuous their pressures on the individual's striving, the more active will tend to be the whole process of pushing toward the goal. The general concept of dramatic action can be put into a nutshell by saying it is *a series of changes experienced in a pursuit of adjustment.*

4. If in prospect or retrospect the experience of a striking change seems to be logically connected with the whole situation one is observing, one recognizes it as being arresting, dramatic. If it cannot be so connected, it is shocking, or at best absurd. The death of a woman by gunfire while she is ministering to her stricken husband can be either dramatic or shocking. It is dramatic if she is in a scene of fighting in which she or her husband has been a participant, shocking if she is in her home and the shots are unrelated and accidental. The falling of a ceiling on a man's head can be dramatic if he is an architect and he designed the room, and if those who remark about the accident later observe that there was a kind of poetic justice in it. The falling ceiling will be undramatic if the man is a casual visitor not emotionally attached in any way to the scene. In

any designed composition dramatic effects must be built on concepts of appropriateness. The use of incongruous factors in a surprise is a stock device of comedy. Even here, however, there must be *some* feeling of fitness or the effect will be merely unpleasant—"silly." In the light of these observations one might define the dramatic effect in art as a *feeling caused by a quick shift between related contrasts* (the opposite poles of the same general experience). As already stated, it is usually based on a change from a state of lower animation to a higher one or the reverse (from "evil" to "good," or "good" to "evil"). The relatedness of the two ends of the change are sensed along with the change itself. Oedipus' fall from his eminence is a progressive one; there are many smaller changes working toward the great one. Every one of them, however, is connected somehow with Oedipus' kingship over Thebes.

5. Feelings of pleasure and unpleasure, and especially the emotions, depend for their existence on quick changes of condition, normally connected with a movement from a sense of lower vitality to a sense of higher vitality or the reverse. One has been shut up in a hot house all day, perhaps, and now has an opportunity to walk out in the cool evening air. One is striding along with pleasure when suddenly one turns one's ankle painfully. A gradual shift from one condition to another causes little depth of feeling because the human organism can adjust itself without much effort to the slow shifts. What puts it into the state of sharp feeling then is whatever demands it to do something (bad or good) for which it is not immediately prepared. A sudden block in the path of good action will cause fear or anger, while a sudden removable of a block to desirable action will cause joy. It is the function of theatre to create feelings by drawing the senses and the imagination of the spectator into just such quick changes.

CHAPTER VI

1. Edmund W. Sinnott, *Cell and Psyche: the Biology of Purpose* (Chapel Hill, N.C.: The University of North Carolina Press, 1950), p. 96.

2. It could be argued with considerable logic that Chekhov's heroes do not belong in the tradition of Myth-Heroes. Their tragedy lies in the fact not that they lack fire but that they lack direction. They have the *emotions* for legend-making but their actions are frustrated before they can get started moving toward a goal.

3. John Steinbeck, *Of Mice and Men* (New York: Covici Friede, 1937), pp. 101, 103-4.

4. "The order of the world is no accident. There is nothing actual which could be actual without some measure of order. The religious insight is the grasp of this truth: That the order of the world, the depth of reality of the world, the value of the world in its whole and in its parts, the beauty of the world, the zest of life, the peace of life, and the mastery of evil, are all bound together—not accidentally, but by reason of this truth: that the universe exhibits a creativity with infinite freedom, and a realm of forms with infinite possibilities; but that this creativity and these forms are together impotent to achieve actuality apart from the completed ideal harmony, which is God."—Alfred North Whitehead,

Religion in the Making (New York: The Macmillan Company, 1926), pp. 119-20.

5. Herbert J. Muller, *Science and Criticism* (New Haven: Yale University Press, 1943), p. 274.

6. Gordon W. Allport, *The Individual and His Religion* (New York: The Macmillan Co., 1952), p. 142.

7. A complaint heard often is that modern playwriting is "anemic"; it wants richness. In it there is no lack of theatricality, for there is plenty of surface excitement, but the blood which runs through the heart of much of the writing is cool. Twenty-four hours after one has seen or read a typical stage work of today one feels no longer stirred by it, and a month later one has just about forgotten it. What is it that causes the feebleness of feeling? It is not a want of interesting character drawing. It is not the absence of skillful dialogue. Yet, somehow, the play lacks fire. Why? Several reasons are frequently cited: a breakdown in common convictions which makes it difficult for the playwright to use any burning moral premise, the rootlessness of whole sections of our citizenship, everyone's preoccupation with passing fads of thinking. The reasons can finally be summed up in the observation that the experience of the usual stage personality as it is revealed to us today is essentially transient. It is tentative, questioning. It tugs at no part of the spectator which belongs to the long stretches of life. In the sufferings and the triumphs of the dramatic hero little is implied about his connection with the age-old tradition of the seasons, the swinging tides of universal forces. Our theatre personalities are active, they are busy, they glitter, and they chatter, but they are impotent. Consequently what we see about the exercising of their emotions is not more than momentarily absorbing.

What these figures lack is an heroic quality. But writers of the schools of "realism" tell us that hero worship is romantic. Man, we are told, does not need to compare his nature with that of superior beings. He does not need to participate in their thoughts and feelings—he cannot do it actually, and he should not try to do it by make-believe. Looking straight into the face of the conditions in which he exists, he should cultivate either a firm self-sufficiency or a dignified resignation. Reaching toward what is outside of oneself is futile "escapism" from the facts of life. What such authors choose not to see is that hero-thinking is a fundamental part of human nature. A man can no more keep himself from putting his mind on images of greatness than he can keep himself from dreaming of success. If he must destroy one hero, he will set up another and attach his own longing soul to the strength in that character. Even the cynic has his heroes, persons who seem to be more steadfast than he in those very negative qualities which he thinks he admires. What he strives to touch (though he will probably not admit it) is not so much the doubts of his hero as his courage to hold the doubts. So what is sought in the end, even by the cynic, is a form of Life, not Death.

CHAPTER VII

1. Playgoing is a social activity. Since any show of what might be interpreted as cowardice (a "defeatist attitude") is generally frowned on

by an assembled herd, human custom demands that public art calling for massed responses shall be positive rather than negative.

2. Edmund W. Sinnott, *Cell and Psyche: the Biology of Purpose* (Chapel Hill, N.C.: The University of North Carolina Press, 1950), pp. 97, 102.

3. Maxwell Anderson, *Off Broadway* (New York: William Sloane Associates, 1947), p. 39.